Roye

Town & Country

From palaces to pubs,
sites of the monarchy
in public and private

the handbook guide

First published in 1997 by
Handbook Publishing Ltd, 14 Anhalt Road, London SW11 4NX

ISBN 1-901309-00-2

Printed in England by Biddles Ltd, Guildford and Kings Lynn

Compiled and edited by Crail Low and Lucy Minto
Book and cover design by Ivan Bulloch

Maps compiled from the 1939 John Bartholomew Atlas revised from copyright
free aerial photography and checked on foot. Drawn and produced by Landfall
Mapping, Southampton (01703) 7300099/585041

Cover Illustration: Elizabeth I © National Portrait Gallery & Andy Warhol Portrait
of Queen Elizabeth II © ARS, NY & DACS, London 1997

Photographs © Crail Low, except: pages 6-7 © Camera Press (Mike Anthony),
31 © Camera Press (The Times 1953), 59 © Camera Press (Charles de la Court),
86 © Camera Press, 123 © National Portrait Gallery, 135 © Camera Press
(Richard Gillard), 136 © Camera Press, 142 © Camera Press (Glenn Harvey),
150 © Camera Press, 152-3 © Camera Press (Jack Esten), 155 © Camera Press,
158 © Camera Press (Colin Davey), 164 © National Portrait Gallery (both),
166 © National Portrait Gallery (picture of George IV) & © Camera Press
(Cecil Beaton - portrait of Elizabeth II), 171 © Martyn Hayhow/PA

Other titles in the series

Rock & Pop London

Forthcoming titles

The River Thames

Villages of London

Gardens & Wildlife in London

Film & TV: Location London

Contents

ROYAL LIFE: Town & Country

The first King of England came to the throne in the late ninth century. Since then, this former outpost of the Roman Empire has seen its sovereignty spread over the continents of North America, Asia, Africa and Australasia. The power has all but gone, yet the memories and ghosts of that splendid past reverberate in buildings, pageantry and symbols.

And the Crown continues, through war, murder, abdication and ridicule. Over forty times, from one reign to the next, from one dynasty to another, the people have cried: 'The monarch is dead; long live the monarch!'

While most countries have thrown out their kings and queens, Britain has retained hers, partly through affection, partly through fear of change. But mostly because the monarchy lies at the heart of the country: in Society, the Church, Government and the Military.

THE HANDBOOK GUIDE TO ROYAL LIFE shows the places they lived, some ruined, others retaining their palatial glory. Though the properties are spread throughout the British Isles, they are mostly located in the south-east along the strategically dominant Thames Valley.

This book is neither a history of, nor an argument for, monarchy. It does not list all the buildings with royal associations, nor every battlefield. But what it does do is show the places that record the life of one of the world's most important and enduring institutions.

THE HANDBOOK GUIDE TO ROYAL LIFE is set out by region and contains detailed information of the everyday life of the present royal family. Of course many of these haunts are public and should you bump into them, please respect their privacy.

Notes on the text

1 Names in heavy type highlight historical monarchs and the present royal family, e.g. **King John** and **Diana, Princess of Wales**, when they are a subject of the entry.

2 Places in heavy type highlight sites with entries elsewhere, e.g. BUCKINGHAM PALACE and BERKHAMPSTED CASTLE.

3 Places in italics highlight an object of interest, which does not have its own separate entry, e.g. *Birdcage Walk* and *Gold State Coach*.

The Royal Family ON THE BALCONY OF **Buckingham Palace**

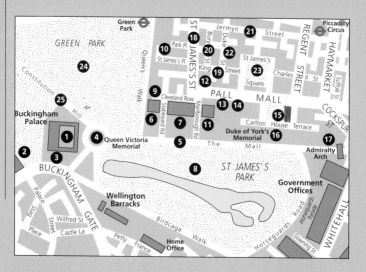

St James

This is the London address of both the Queen and her heir, Prince Charles. It is famous for the grand houses and shops which sprang up around the two palaces, St James's and Buckingham. Many other members of the royal family live in St James, making it London's 'Royal Village'.

1 | BUCKINGHAM PALACE SW1
Tel. (0171) 839 1377
Open Aug-Sept: daily 9.00am-4.15pm
Admission charge
Buckingham Palace is the official English residence of the Queen. It is also her London home.

THE HISTORY
Until the early seventeenth century, the site was a garden of thirty thousand Mulberry trees for the silkworm factories of **James I**.

The 'Keeper of the Mulberry Trees' was Lord Goring and it was he who first built a modest mansion, Goring House, on the land. Later, the property was leased to the Earl of Arlington. His wife introduced tea to London Society when, in the drawing room of the revamped Arlington House, she brewed the first pot in England.

The Duke of Buckingham took over the lease and after a fire in 1703, built one of the grandest houses of its time in London: Buckingham House.

In 1762, **George III** bought Buckingham House for the then vast sum of £28,000. The king was a private man and intended the house to be his retreat from the nearby pressures of court life at ST JAMES'S PALACE.

However, after George became ill in 1775, his wife, Charlotte, lived here alone and it became known as 'the Queen's House'.

George IV made extensive alterations and extensions using the fashionable London architect, John Nash. This upgraded the grand house into a palace. But unfortunately George died before he could move in.

BUCKINGHAM PALACE THE ROYAL COAT OF ARMS ON THE GATES

In spite of the grandeur, the finished building was unhealthy to live in. Its vast spaces were cold, badly ventilated and diseases like typhoid flourished. For this reason, **William IV's** court remained at **St James's Palace**. He even offered Buckingham Palace as a replacement for the Houses of Parliament, recently destroyed by fire. The politicians declined and the palace was left empty.

It was only when **Queen Victoria** made further alterations that Buckingham Palace became the official residence of the monarchy in England.

THE TWENTIETH CENTURY

During the Second World War, the palace was bombed twice. In spite of this, the royal family remained living here. In so doing, they gained much love and affection from the public for sharing their suffering. Indeed **the Queen Mother** said, 'at last, I can look the East-end in the face.'

Prince Charles was born in 1948 on the first floor overlooking the Mall. He was born at the palace because, until the 1960s, no member of the royal family ever attended hospital. Even his grandfather, **George VI**, when his cancerous left lung was removed in 1951, had the operation in a specially converted room at the palace.

ROYAL LIFE

Life in Buckingham Palace is structured and almost timeless. The routine and uses of the 19 state rooms, 52 bedrooms, 92 offices, 98 bathrooms, post office, entertainment and sports facilities have not changed dramatically since Victorian times.

In the nineteenth century there were no less than 200 footmen and 100 cooks. Modern equipment has lessened the need for servants and today there are 13 footmen, 36 housemaids, 17 cooks, and 7 porters amongst the two hundred domestic staff. However, no more than twelve have daily contact with the Queen.

The Queen and Prince Philip have their suite of twelve rooms, on the first floor of the north wing overlooking **Green Park**.

The east wing, which hides much of the original palace, is used for the private apartments of her children. The central balcony overlooking **the Mall** is where the royal family acknowledge the crowds on state occasions.

THE QUEEN'S ROUTINE:
Morning

The Queen is awoken with a cup of tea at 7.30am in her bedroom before joining the Duke of Edinburgh for breakfast.

She arrives in her office at 9.30am. For the first hour, she:
■ attends to royal business ■ reads parliamentary reports ■ reads a digest of the day's news ■ sends centenary telegrams (4,000 in 1996) ■ deals with correspondence (at the start of her reign it was 300 letters a year, today it is over 300,000)

At 10.30am the Queen leaves the office to attend to royal duties elsewhere in the palace. These can include:
■ monthly meeting of the Privy Council (Privy Councillors are politicians who advise the monarch) ■ receptions, including those for new ambassadors
■ ceremonies, including investitures.

Before lunch, the Queen walks her dogs in the gardens. Her father owned the first Corgi in 1933 and it has been the Queen's favourite breed ever since.

Afternoon
After a simple lunch at 1.00pm, taken either in private or with a guest, the Queen will carry out appointments in and around London. In summer, garden parties are held for up to two thousand people from around the country.

If the Queen has no other business, she will take tea at 4.00pm. Tea nearly always consists of cucumber sandwiches and a slice of Dundee cake.

Evening
When alone, the Queen will eat dinner from a tray in her private sitting room and watch television. More often she is required to dine formally at an engagement in London.

For state banquets, the palace will spare no effort or expense. Days are spent polishing and laying tables with menus always written in French. Every year, £37,000 is spent on floral decorations.

Throughout the day, a member of the police force's royal unit will remain discretely near the Queen. At night after she retires to bed, the policeman will put on purpose-made slippers so as to lessen any noise and stay outside her door.

Each Friday, the Queen will leave Buckingham Palace after lunch to be driven the twenty-five miles to spend the weekend at **WINDSOR CASTLE**, where she remains until early Monday afternoon.

The Changing of the Guards
April-July: daily 11.30am (Aug-April alternate days)
The changing of the guard takes place inside the gates of Buckingham Palace. The new guard marches behind its regimental band from Wellington Barracks, in Birdcage Walk, to the forecourt of the palace, where the sentries change over.

The ceremony can also be seen at **ST JAMES'S PALACE** (daily 11.15am) and at **HORSE GUARDS** (daily 11.00am except Sun 10.00am) when the mounted Household Cavalry ride along the Mall before and after.

Trooping the Colour
15 June each year at Horse Guards Parade
The trooping of the colour originates from an ancient military custom, which taught soldiers loyalty to their warlord and identified their fighting flag. This was important when in the chaos of war, they needed to know where to rally around their leader.

The ceremony has been held regularly from 1805 on the monarch's official birthday. In the present Queen's case, 15 June, the day of her coronation in 1953.

The Queen is Commander-in-Chief of the Armed Forces and, during the ceremony, witnesses the raising of the regiments' flags (colours). She used to attend the ceremony side-saddle, but since an assassination attempt in 1981, she uses an open horse-drawn carriage.

2 | **ROYAL MEWS** Buckingham Palace Road SW1

Tel. (0171) 930 4832

Open Tue-Thur 12-4pm (Oct-Dec: Wed only)

Closed during Royal Ascot Week in June & State occasions

Admission charge

The Royal Mews garages the Queen's horse-drawn carriages and cars. The complex houses the four most important royal coaches:

- The *Gold State Coach* first used by **George III** in 1762
- The *Irish Coach* used by **Queen Victoria** for the State Opening of Parliament
- The *Open State Landau* built for **Edward VII** and used for foreign state visits
- The *Glass Coach* built in 1910 for **George V** and used for royal weddings

Five coachmen and fifteen grooms work at the Mews and look after the thirty horses.

3 | **QUEEN'S GALLERY** Buckingham Palace Road SW1

Tel. (0171) 930 4832

Open daily 9.30am-4.00pm

Admission charge

The Queen's Gallery exhibits from the Crown's collection of pictures and works of art. The collection was started by the Tudor monarchs and is one of the greatest in the world.

The Queen opened the gallery in 1962 in Queen Victoria's war-damaged chapel. During the Second World War, bombing damaged much of the surrounding west wing.

4 | **QUEEN VICTORIA MEMORIAL**

The Mall SW1

The statue by sculptor, Thomas Brock, was completed in 1911 as a memorial to **Queen Victoria**. Made from 2,300 tonnes of marble, it represents the glory of the Empire and the virtues exulted during her reign: charity, truth and justice are shown alongside shipbuilding, war, manufacturing and progress. And of course, Victoria soars above them all.

5 | **THE MALL** SW1

The Mall started out as little more than a country lane. **Charles II** lined it with trees and it became a fashionable promenade after he opened **ST JAMES'S PARK** to the public.

THE QUEEN VICTORIA MEMORIAL

Only in 1910 was the Mall turned into a formal ceremonial road as part of the Queen Victoria memorial scheme.

THE MALL LOOKING TOWARDS BUCKINGHAM PALACE

ROYAL AMBUSH
Princess Anne was ambushed outside **CLARENCE HOUSE** on 20th March 1974.
She was returning with her husband from a dinner engagement when her car
was blocked by a white Ford Escort. Its driver, Ian Ball, intended to kidnap and
ransom the princess for £3 million.

Ball attempted to drag Anne from her car. During the struggle, her private
detective, James Heaton, was shot three times.

Ball was subsequently sent to Rampton Hospital for the Criminally Insane.
Both Heaton and the princess received medals for bravery.

6 | CLARENCE HOUSE The Mall SW1
Private
Clarence House was built in the grounds of **ST JAMES'S PALACE** in 1828 by John
Nash and was named after its first resident, the Duke of Clarence (later **William
IV**). As king, he continued to live here both for his comfort and because his vast
collection of books would not fit into **ST JAMES'S**.

Queen Victoria moved her mother, the Duchess of Kent, to Clarence House
from their former home at **KENSINGTON PALACE**. The duchess remained here until
her death in 1861. Clarence House was then home to two of Victoria's sons,
Prince Alfred and Prince Arthur.

THE TWENTIETH CENTURY
Clarence House was the first home of Princess Elizabeth and Prince Philip after
they married in 1947. The building had been used by the Red Cross during the
Second World War and £50,000 needed to be spent refurbishing their twenty-
roomed apartment on the first and second floors. Their second child, **Princess
Anne**, was born on 15th August 1950 in the apartment.

After the death of her father **George VI**, Elizabeth II moved to **BUCKINGHAM
PALACE** and since 1953 **the Queen Mother** has lived in Clarence House.

Princess Margaret shared the house with her mother until 1961.

CLARENCE HOUSE VIEW FROM THE MALL

In the 1950s Clarence House was the site of the first modern royal scandal when Margaret had an affair with Peter Townshend. Though an equerry to the king, Townshend was divorced with two children and Margaret would have had to give up her royal position and benefits to marry him. She was unable to and amid much newspaper coverage she ended the relationship. Margaret's decision was relayed to the BBC, where programmes were interrupted for the announcement.

However, the princess continued to cause scandal. She remained very much part of London society, attending parties and fashionable night clubs with various male friends, one of whom was a society photographer, Anthony Armstrong-Jones.

He was without a title and as their relationship developed, the Queen came to terms with the fact that her sister would marry a commoner. In 1961 the wedding was televised throughout the world and helped to promote a more modern image of the royal family. The couple moved into an apartment in **KENSINGTON PALACE**.

Since then, only the Queen Mother has used Clarence House, except for a short period in 1981 when **Diana Spencer** stayed to prepare for her marriage.

Clarence House given to Prince Charles 2002

7 | ST JAMES'S PALACE SW1
Private
THE HISTORY

St James's Palace stands on the site of a leper hospital run by the Sisters of St James-in-the-Fields.

Henry VIII dissolved the religious order in the 1530s and demolished the hospital. In its place he built a palace. The Tudor gate-house and three of the original courts remain: Friary, Ambassadors and Colour Courts. Henry never lived at St James's, preferring **WHITEHALL PALACE** when in London. However, it was here that he died in 1547, much bloated and in great pain after suffering for many years from open ulcers.

His daughter **Mary I** made St James's her home. She disliked the cold grandeur of Whitehall and only used it for state occasions. Mary died of influenza at St James's in 1558.

After **WHITEHALL** burnt down in 1698, St James's became the official royal residence. **Queen Anne** spent much of each year at the palace where she gave birth to most of her seventeen children.

The Hanoverian kings made the palace the centre of London society in the early eighteenth century.

The modest **George III**, however, slowly moved his family to the newly purchased Buckingham House. He was the first to try and make a distinction

ST JAMES'S PALACE THE TUDOR GATEHOUSE

between the monarch's private and public lives. Thus he often used the separate buildings for different functions.

After **William IV**'s death in 1837, the seat of the monarch moved to **BUCKINGHAM PALACE**. St James's was subsequently divided into apartments for members of the royal family.

THE TWENTIETH CENTURY

The Duke of York (later **George V**) lived in *York House*, the seventy-five roomed west wing of the palace, before he became king. The Queen's cousin, the Duke of Kent, lives in York House today.

Prince Charles maintains an apartment here. In addition he has recently moved his offices to St James' after many years at **BUCKINGHAM PALACE**.

Charles attends to his various duties from this office. Apart from being patron of numerous charities and organisations, he is also ceremonial head of several military bodies.

Though the Prince of Wales is his senior title, he is also known as the Duke of Cornwall and when in Scotland, the Duke of Rothesay. Rothesay is the oldest dukedom in Scotland and was created in 1398 by the Scots King **Robert III**. Since then it has always been used by the heir to the Scottish Crown.

Ceremony of Accession

From the balcony of Friary Court, each new reign is proclaimed. This ceremony is accompanied by a heralds' fanfare, repeated at Charing Cross and Temple Bar, on the boundary with the City of London.

St James's Park

THE CHAPEL ROYAL

(Services held on Sundays in winter)

The Chapel Royal has been at St James's Palace since 1702.

The most famous service of the Chapel Royal is that of the Epiphany on 6th January. During this seven hundred year old service a representative of the Sovereign makes an offering of gold to the poor. **George II** was the last to take part personally in the ceremony.

Many royal marriages have taken place in the chapel:

■ William, Prince of Orange and his cousin, Mary Stuart (later **William III** and **Mary II**) married at the chapel in 1677.

■ The Prince Regent (later **George IV**) was forced to marry his cousin, Caroline of Brunswick, in exchange for parliament settling his debts. The marriage took place in the chapel in 1795. The Prince became so drunk that he spent his wedding night collapsed in the fireplace of the bridal chamber in the palace.

■ **Queen Victoria** married Prince Albert on 10th February 1840: the ceremony took place at the unusual time of 1.00pm, for until then most royal weddings had taken place at night. It rained all day and after a modest banquet at **Buckingham Palace**, the couple honeymooned for three days at **Windsor Castle**.

■ Her grandson, the Duke of York (later **George V),** married Princess Mary of Teck, his poor royal relation. As goddaughter of Queen Victoria and granddaughter of George III, Mary had first been engaged to George's elder brother, the Duke of Clarence. However he died at **Sandringham**, leaving George to take his place.

8 | ST JAMES'S PARK The Mall SW1

Tel. (0171) 930 1793

Open daily 5am-dusk

Free

The land became the first royal park when fields surrounding the leper hospital of St James were enclosed by **Henry VIII** in 1532. The swamp land was drained to prevent flooding by the rivers Thames and Tyburn.

Later monarchs slowly developed the park:

■ **James I** kept his collection of exotic animals here.

■ **Charles II** redesigned the park inspired by the gardens at Versailles, outside Paris. After creating lawns, building the canal and planting trees, Charles opened the park to the public. *Birdcage Walk* was named after the aviary he established there. Birds are still a feature of the park, particularly the pelicans originally donated by the Russian Ambassador in the eighteenth century.

■ Early in the nineteenth century, **George IV** ordered John Nash to re-landscape the park. Nash removed the 'French' characteristics to give a more 'English' appearance: the canal became a lake and informality replaced formality.

■ **Queen Victoria** gave the park an increased focus, when she moved the royal residence from St James's to Buckingham Palace.

During the First World War, the lake was drained to provide space for temporary offices. Today, the park is a quiet retreat in the centre of London.

Lancaster House seen from Green Park

9 | LANCASTER HOUSE Stable Yard Road SW1
Private
The present house was built in 1825 for the brother of **George IV**, the Duke of York. Unfortunately the house was not completed at the time of his death and the lease was sold to the Duke of Sutherland to settle his gambling debts.

The house was named Lancaster House in 1912 by Viscount Leverhulme (founder of the Unilever soap empire) after his home county. In his will, he left the house to the nation.

Elizabeth II's coronation banquet was held at Lancaster House in 1953.

10 | SPENCER HOUSE 27 St James's Place SW1
Tel. (0171) 499 8620
Open Sun 10.30am-4.30pm (closed Aug & Jan)
Admission charge
The house was built between 1756-1766 for the first Earl Spencer by architect
John Vardy. **Diana, Princess of Wales**, is the sister of the present earl. The
house is leased to Lord Rothschild.

SPENCER HOUSE DIANA'S ANCESTRAL LONDON HOME

11 | MARLBOROUGH HOUSE Pall Mall SW1
Private
Marlborough House was built in 1709 by Sarah, Duchess of Marlborough. She
was given a long lease on land belonging to St James's Palace by her close friend,
Queen Anne. The duchess commissioned Christopher Wren, architect of **ST
PAUL'S CATHEDRAL**, to design the building.

When the lease reverted to the Crown in 1817, **George III** gave the house to
his granddaughter, Princess Charlotte and her husband, Prince Leopold of
Belgium. Though Charlotte died in childbirth later that year, Leopold remained
here until he became King of Belgium in 1831.

The house then passed to Queen Adelaide, the widow of **William IV**.

Perhaps the most famous period was when the Prince of Wales (later **Edward
VII**) lived here, from 1863-1901. **Queen Victoria** had made Marlborough House
the official residence of the Prince of Wales by an Act of Parliament and for
nearly forty years, Edward and his wife, Princess Alexandra, made it the glittering
centre of London Society.

The prince was notorious for his string of thirteen known mistresses and his
love of gambling. Close friends became part of 'the Marlborough Circle'. His
mistresses would call at the house and some were even received by Princess
Alexandra.

George V was born in Marlborough House and lived here as Prince of Wales from 1903-1910. On his accession to the throne, it was home again to his mother, the widowed Queen Alexandra. She lived here until her death in 1924.

The last royal resident was Queen Mary, widow of George V, on whose death in 1953, the house was leased to the Commonwealth.

12 | MARLBOROUGH CLUB 52 Pall Mall SW1
Private

The Marlborough Club was created by the Prince of Wales (later **Edward VII**) in 1869. He opened the club after resigning from *White's*, at 37 St James's Street, because the club rules would not allow him to smoke in the morning room. Edward was addicted to tobacco and smoked twelve Cuban cigars and countless cigarettes each day.

The Marlborough Club was intended for the use of his friends with the large billiards room the centre of activity. The club closed in 1952.

13 | NELL GWYNNE'S HOUSE 79 Pall Mall SW1
Private

Home to Nell Gwynne, the mistress of **Charles II**.

The former actress was given the property freehold in 1676, after refusing to live on leasehold land: "I have always conveyed myself *free* to the Crown", she said.

On her death in 1687 the house passed to their son, the Duke of St Albans.

ROYAL MARRIAGE SCANDAL
A scandal was caused in the mid-eighteenth century when **George III**'s brother, the Duke of Gloucester, secretly married a Catholic, the Dowager Countess of Waldgrave, in the sitting room of the house.

The marriage, along with that of his younger brother, the Duke of Cumberland, to a divorcee, Mrs Anne Horton, led to the 1772 Royal Marriages Act. This Act prevented heirs to the throne marrying without the consent of the Sovereign. It followed on from the 1701 Act of Settlement which already forbade an heir to the throne marrying a Catholic so as to ensure a Protestant succession.

Charles II housed another mistress, Barbara Villiers, in Pall Mall, on the site of *Bridgewater House, Cleveland Row*. She lived there from 1668, before moving to Chiswick in the 1680s.

They had three sons. The Duke of Southampton was given land around Cleveland Street W1 and the Duke of Grafton inherited land around Tottenham Court Road W1. At the age of nine Grafton married the five-year-old daughter of Lord Arlington (who at the time owned house on the site of BUCKINGHAM PALACE).

14 | PALL MALL SW1

The name of the street comes from **Charles II**'s favourite game, pell-mell. This was a mix of English croquet and French boules. The king first played pell-mell in ST JAMES'S PARK.

In June 1807, to celebrate the birthday of **George III**, Pall Mall became the first road in England to be lit by gas.

Other Sites:
77-78 Pall Mall
Private

Home, in the past, to various members of the royal family. Residents have included Princess Christian, daughter of **Queen Victoria**, who lived at the house from 1902-23. Her daughters then lived in the house until 1947.

105 Pall Mall
Private

Home to Maria Fitzherbert, the wife of the Prince Regent (later **George IV),** who lived here from 1789-1796.

They had married in *Park Street*, Mayfair in 1785. The wedding was conducted in secret because marriage between the heir to the throne and a Catholic was illegal. Despite this, the prince had insisted upon the marriage, even threatening suicide until Fitzherbert became his wife.

Later, when the prince needed to marry Caroline of Brunswick in exchange for settlement of his financial debts, all evidence of the marriage was destroyed. However, they remained close and Mrs Fitzherbert nursed him during the last years of his life.

CARLTON HOUSE TERRACE VIEW FROM THE MALL

15 | CARLTON HOUSE TERRACE SW1

This row of grand houses marks the site of Carlton House, demolished in 1820.

Lord Carlton's original house stood in the grounds of **ST JAMES'S PALACE**. In 1732, his family sold the house to Frederick, the Prince of Wales and wayward heir of **George II**.

Carlton House then became the setting for the rivalry between their two courts.

Until his death in 1751, Frederick intentionally embarrassed his father by mirroring the king's court at St James's: every celebration, ceremony and dinner that the king held, was rivalled or bettered at Carlton House by his son.

In 1783, the site was revived when **George III** gave Carlton House to his son, the new Prince of Wales.

The prince (later **George IV)** made extravagant alterations to the property turning it into London's grandest house, where the 'batchelor' prince held court to London Society.

But he was unable to pay the bills. In 1795 his debts totalled over £500,000 and he was forced to reach a deal with parliament: in return for marrying his distant and obscene German cousin, Caroline of Brunswick, the nation would settle his debts.

But marriage did not curb his extravagant lifestyle, particularly after 1811 when, due to the king's madness, he became Prince Regent.

Carlton House became his court and grandiose plans for building were made here: including the remodelling of **REGENT STREET**, his palaces in **BRIGHTON** and **REGENT'S PARK**.

State banquets and balls were held regularly. Kings and emperors were entertained. In 1814, perhaps the largest ball took place for the Duke of Wellington, prior to his victory at the Battle of Waterloo.

When he ascended the throne in 1820 as **George IV**, he had no further use for the house and ordered its demolition. The best parts were retained for use elsewhere: twenty-three chimneys and the parquetry floors went to the new royal apartments at **WINDSOR CASTLE**, with other furnishings going to **BUCKINGHAM PALACE**. Some of the colonnades went to the new art gallery at **TRAFALGAR SQUARE**.

16 | DUKE OF YORK'S MEMORIAL Waterloo Place SW1

At the end of Waterloo Place stands the statue to **George III**'s second son. He was the 'Grand Old Duke of York' of the children's nursery rhyme.

The duke was Commander-in-Chief of the army but resigned after his mistress was accused of selling army commissions and promotions.

The statue was funded by the army when each soldier was deducted a day's pay. As the duke died £2 million in debt, it was built so tall to prevent creditors defacing his memorial.

17 | ADMIRALTY ARCH

Admiralty Arch divides **THE MALL** from **TRAFALGAR SQUARE**. It was built in 1910 as part of the scheme to commemorate **Queen Victoria** and was used as the administrative headquarters of the navy.

The gate in the centre is only opened for the monarch on ceremonial occasions.

SHOPPING IN ST JAMES'S

There are many shops in St James's that hold a royal warrant. Royal warrants are issued by the Queen, the Duke of Edinburgh, the Prince of Wales or the Queen Mother. The warrant signifies that the shop has been used by the royal family for at least three years.

There are many shops in the area which do not hold a warrant but are frequented by the royal family.

BERRY BROS

18 | ST JAMES'S STREET SW1
Berry Brothers & Rudd Ltd 3 St James's Street
One of the oldest wine shops in the country.
James Lock & Co. 6 St James's Street
The Queen has all her hats made here.
John Lobb 9 St James's Street SW1
Shoemaker to the royal family since 1911.
Truefitt & Hill 71 St James's Street SW1
The Dukes of Edinburgh and Kent have had their hair cut by Mr Wilson for over forty years. He also cut the hair of Winston Churchill and Prince Michael of Kent.

19 | KING STREET SW1
Spink & Sons 5-7 King Street
Medal-makers for ranks of chivalry since 1666.

20 | BURY STREET SW1
Paul Longmire 12 Bury Street
Antique dealer. Prince Charles bought Diana her 21st Birthday present, a brooch of a plume of feathers, from the shop.

TURNBULL & ASSER

22

PAXTON &
WHITFIELD

FLORIS

21 | JERMYN STREET SW1

Hawes & Curtis 23 Jermyn Street
Prince Charles buys suits from these
tailors.

Trickers 67 Jermyn Street
Prince Charles has shoes made here.
He was recommended the shoe-
makers by ex-brother-in-law, Charles
Althorp, Earl Spencer.

Turnbull & Asser 70 Jermyn Street
Prince Charles has his shirts made here
by Paul Cuss. Michael Caine and
Warren Christopher, the ex-US
Secretary of State, are frequent
customers. Diana has also bought
shirts here.

J Floris 89 Jermyn Street
Perfumery supplying toiletries to the
royal family. Prince Charles gets his
eau-de-colognes from the shop.

Paxton & Whitfield 93 Jermyn Street
Established in 1797, this is the oldest
cheese shop in Britain. It has the
Queen Mother's warrant.

22 | PRINCES' GALLERIES 10 Duke Street SW1

The royal family has a long connection with the Freemasons. The Duke of Edinburgh is a mason and the Duke of Kent is the Grandmaster.

On the 2nd December 1919, the Duke of York (later **George VI**) was initiated into the Freemasons' United Royal Arch at these galleries.

23 | ST JAMES'S SQUARE SW1
17 St James's Square
Private

Home to Queen Caroline. Her husband, **George IV**, disliked her intensely and refused her entry to his coronation in 1820 much to the fury of the nation.

She lived here during the king's attempt to divorce her for adultery. Caroline would ride daily from the house to the House of Lords for investigation, cheered on by the large crowds.

20 St James's Square
Private

London home of Elizabeth Bowes-Lyon (later **the Queen Mother**) from 1906-1920.

Before her marriage to the Duke of York (later **George VI**), Elizabeth was one of the most desirable debutantes of her generation.

21 St James's Square
Private

No. 21 was built on the site of a house used by the Catholic **James II** to accommodate two unpopular mistresses: Arabella Churchill and Catherine Sedley. The court joked that these two women had been forced on the king by his priests as penance for his sins.

31 St James's Square
Private

George III was born here on 4th June 1738. His father, the Prince of Wales, rented the house after he had been evicted from **ST JAMES'S PALACE** by **George II**. The Prince and his family lived here whilst waiting for the completion of **CARLTON HOUSE**.

24 | GREEN PARK SW1
Tel. (0171) 930 1793
Open daily 5am-dusk
Free

Green Park was originally meadow-land where duels were fought. Lying north-west of **ST JAMES'S PALACE**, the park was named after the 'green' of the meadows.

The meadows were the scene of several uprisings and battles:
■ In 1554, Sir Thomas Wyatt led an army rebellion against the unpopular decision of **Mary I** to marry the Catholic King Philip of Spain.
■ During the Civil War in England nearly a hundred years later, the Parliamentarians fortified the meadows to defend against Royalist attacks.

Charles II enclosed the land to make it a royal park. True to his extravagant lifestyle he built an icehouse to cool drinks in the summer. The park was, like **St James's Park**, open to the public allowing Charles the freedom to walk amongst his subjects.

Queen's Walk, along the eastern boundary of the park, was named after the wife of **George II**, Queen Caroline. She created the pathway for her private use and built a pavilion where she would take breakfast. In January 1737 whilst eating in the pavilion she caught a chill and died ten days later.

Alterations were made to Green Park in honour of **Queen Victoria**. The *Broad Walk* was created as a walkway down to the **Queen Victoria Memorial** outside **Buckingham Palace**. The gates at the end of the Broad Walk celebrate the Commonwealth countries: Canada, Australiasia and South Africa.

25 | CONSTITUTION HILL SW1

Constitution Hill was named after the regular morning 'constitutional' walks of **Charles II**.

ROYAL ASSASSINATION ATTEMPT
When **Queen Victoria** first came to the throne, her Prime Minister was Lord Melbourne. He made little provision for the increased poverty of the working classes. This caused social unrest and Victoria became a focus for it as she was thought to be too close to the Prime Minister. Indeed she was often mocked as 'Mrs Melbourne'. More dangerously, several people attempted to assassinate her.

The first took place here, on Constitution Hill one evening in June 1840 when Edward Oxford fired two shots at her open carriage.

And again in May 1850, when William Hamilton fired one shot at the queen before being arrested.

THE PALACE OF WESTMINSTER

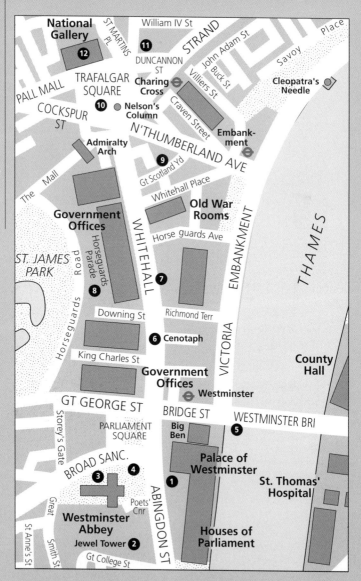

National Gallery

ST MARTINS PL

William IV St

STRAND

12

11

DUNCANNON ST

John Adam St

St Buck St

Savoy Place

Cleopatra's Needle

TRAFALGAR SQUARE

Charing Cross

Villiers St

PALL MALL

COCKSPUR ST

10 Nelson's Column

Craven Street

Embank-ment

N'THUMBERLAND AVE

Admiralty Arch

9

Gt Scotland Yd

Whitehall Place

Old War Rooms

The Mall

Government Offices

Horse guards Ave

THAMES

ST. JAMES PARK

Horseguards Parade

WHITEHALL

EMBANKMENT

8

Horseguards Road

Downing St

Richmond Terr

7

6 Cenotaph

King Charles St

VICTORIA

County Hall

Government Offices

GT GEORGE ST

Westminster

BRIDGE ST

WESTMINSTER BRI

Storey's Gate

PARLIAMENT SQUARE

Big Ben

5

3 **4**

BROAD SANC.

Great Smith St

St Anne's St

Palace of Westminster

1

St. Thomas' Hospital

Poets' Cnr

ABINGDON ST

Westminster Abbey

Jewel Tower **2**

Gt College St

Houses of Parliament

Westminster & Whitehall

The area around Westminster and Whitehall has settlements dating back to Saxon times. Originally it was marsh, dotted with islands of farmland. Today the City of Westminster is home to the seats of both government and monarchy.

1 | PALACE OF WESTMINSTER Parliament Square SW1

Tel. House of Lords (0171) 219 3107

House of Commons (0171) 219 4272

Public access to the Visitor's Gallery of both the Lords and the Commons is free. The Palace of Westminster has been the seat of government for over a thousand years, through both the monarch and Parliament.

THE HISTORY

Westminster was first built on Thorney Island and housed a Benedictine Abbey. It was known as the Minster in the West to distinguish it from **ST PAUL'S CATHEDRAL** in the City.

In the tenth century, after an attack by the Danes, the abbey was rebuilt by **King Edward the Confessor**, who added the first royal palace at Westminster.

In 1099 **William II** built *Westminster Hall* onto the palace as a meeting place for his Council, an early form of parliament. This large space was extended and given its magnificent hammer-beam roof two centuries later by **Richard II**.

STATUE OF **OLIVER CROMWELL** LEADER OF THE PARLIAMENTARIANS AGAINST CHARLES I

During the reign of **Stephen**, the *White Hall* and *St Stephen's Chapel* were added. In 1275, these became the first meeting places for the Commons and the Lords respectively.

When **Henry VIII** moved in 1532 to his new palace at **WHITEHALL**, the Commons and the Lords were granted Westminster as their permanent home. Since then, the monarch has only visited on ceremonial occasions.

CONSPIRATORS CAUGHT

On 5th November 1605, in a cellar beneath the House of Lords, Guy Fawkes and a group of Roman Catholic conspirators were caught with barrels of gunpowder. Their aim was to restore the outlawed Catholic faith by blowing up the Protestant parliament when **James I** was visiting. Guy Fawkes was tortured before his execution, as were the other members of the Gunpowder Plot.

His execution is celebrated each year on 5th November when fireworks and bonfires are lit around the country. And the cellars of Westminster are ceremoniously searched.

Westminster Hall was used for state trials until 1806 when the court moved to the Royal Courts of Justice on the Strand. The most famous trial was that of **Charles I** who was sentenced to death by the court in January 1649.

Westminster Hall is often used as the place where monarchs lie in state after their death.

On 16th October 1834, a fire destroyed most of the Palace of Westminster. Only the Hall, St Stephen's Chapel, its cloisters and the JEWEL TOWER survived. The new parliament building was designed by Charles Barry and Augustus Pugin, in Victorian High Gothic style.

Today, the Houses of Parliament remain in the Palace of Westminster. Each November the Queen opens the new session of parliament from the House of Lords. The Queen always enters in the State Coach through her own entrance at the west end of the palace.

Monarchs have not entered the Commons since 1642, when, just before the start of the Civil War, **Charles I** went to the Commons and demanded the arrest of five members. He was refused. And this challenge to his authority led to the king fleeing London to fight for several years against the Parliamentarian forces.

THE JEWEL TOWER EDWARD III'S TREASURE HOUSE

2 | THE JEWEL TOWER Abingdon Street SW1
Tel. (0171) 222 2219
Open daily 10am-1pm & 2-6pm (Oct-March: closes at 4pm)
Admission charge
The Jewel Tower was built by **Edward III** in 1365 to house his treasure. Formerly it had been kept at Winchester, once London's rival as the seat of power. Originally a moat surrounded the tower, the floor of which can be seen.

The Jewel Tower holds a permanent exhibition of the history of the Houses of Parliament.

WESTMINSTER ABBEY
ELIZABETH II'S
CORONATION IN 1953

3 | WESTMINSTER ABBEY Dean's Yard SW1
Tel. (0171) 222 5152
Open daily 7.30am-6.00pm (Wed closes at 7.45pm)
Free
Ring for details of opening times and costs of visiting Royal Chapels, Chapter House, Museum & Garden
The original Saxon church was rebuilt as a Benedictine Abbey by **Edward the Confessor**. His huge abbey was completed in 1065.

Henry III began to rebuild the east-end to centralise the abbey around the tomb of Edward, who had been canonised in 1163.

The abbey underwent various additions and changes through the years.
Elizabeth I changed its name for a short period in 1560 to the Collegiate Church of St Peter.

Its present design was completed in the mid-eighteenth century when the architect, John Hawksmoor, added the two western towers.

THE CORONATION   Henry III?
? Every monarch has been crowned at Westminster Abbey since **William I** on Christmas Day 1066. The only exceptions are **Edward V**, who died, and **Edward VIII**, who abdicated, before their coronations took place.

The ceremony has remained much the same since that of **Edgar**, who was crowned outside Bath Abbey in 973AD.

However, coronations have not always passed smoothly.
■ During **William I**'s, a riot began when the congregation cheered in French and English. This confused the Norman soldiers guarding outside. Nervous, and believing themselves attacked, they set fire to several houses and charged the crowds. The congregation fled in the mayhem, leaving William the Conqueror alone with the clergy to complete the service.
■ The coronation of **Charles I** was almost ruined when the congregation failed to voice their recognition of the monarch. They did not understand the service and so an ominous silence took place instead of their agreement.

■ During the coronation of **George III**, the congregation ate and drank so noisily that much of the ceremony was drowned by their talk and laughter.

■ The day of **George IV**'s coronation was so hot and the robes he wore so heavy, that he staggered, barely able to walk. He made a grotesque sight as sweat caused his thick make-up to run down his face.

■ **Queen Victoria**'s coronation was unrehearsed. The coronation robe was far too big for her five foot frame; the ring was forced onto the wrong finger; and when given the heavy orb, she nearly dropped it.

The Turkish Ambassador was amazed by the ceremony's pomp and called out, "all this for a woman?"

ROYAL MARRIAGES

■ The wedding of the Duke of York (later **George VI**) to Lady Elizabeth Bowes-Lyon (later **the Queen Mother**) was the first royal wedding in six hundred years not to take place in a private chapel. The couple invited three thousand guests to the abbey and a million people lined the streets. The wedding was also significant as **George VI** was the first in over two hundred years to marry someone without royal blood.

■ Princess Elizabeth (later **Elizabeth II**) married Prince Philip at the abbey on 20th November 1947.

■ Princess Margaret married Anthony Armstrong-Jones on 6th June 1960.

■ Princess Anne and Captain Mark Philips married on 14th November 1973.

■ Prince Andrew and Sarah Ferguson married on 23rd July 1986.

MAUNDY MONDAY

The Royal Maundy ceremony is held every year on Easter Monday at Westminster Abbey. Although it used to take place wherever the Sovereign was in residence.

The ceremony dates back to the twelfth century when **Henry I**'s wife, 'Good Queen Maud', would wash and kiss the feet of the poor in memory of the Last Supper of Jesus.

Elizabeth I changed the ceremony to include a gift of money. **William and Mary** were the last monarchs to kiss the feet and **George V** revived the ceremony after many years of neglect.

BURIAL PLACE

The abbey is the burial place for many monarchs:

■ **Edward the Confessor**

■ **Henry III**

■ **Edward I** and his queen, Eleanor of Castille

■ **Edward III** and his queen, Phillipa

■ **Richard II**, who starved to death at Pontefract Castle after being forced to abdicate by **Henry IV**. (He was first buried at King's Langley but was moved to Westminster by **Henry V**, who is also buried here.)

■ **Henry VII** with his wife, Elizabeth of York

■ The bodies of **Edward IV** and his brother, murdered in the Tower of London

■ **Henry VIII's** wife, Anne of Cleves   unproven

■ **Edward VI**

■ **Mary I**

■ **Elizabeth I**

- **James I** and his mother, **Mary Queen of Scots**
- **Charles II**
- **William and Mary**
- **Anne** with her seventeen children, only one of whom survived beyond infancy
- **George II** in 1760 after a heart-attack at **Westminster Palace**.

Since then monarchs have been buried at **St George's Chapel** in Windsor or **Frogmore Mausoleum**.

4 | ST MARGARET'S CHURCH
Westminster Abbey SW1
Tel. (0171) 222 4027
In this parish church of Westminster, **Henry VIII** married his first wife, Catherine of Aragon, in 1509. This was the first of his six marriages.

In 1994, Lady Sarah Armstrong Jones, daughter of Princess Margaret, married Daniel Chatto here.

5 | STATUE OF BOADICEA
Westminster Bridge SW1
The warrior queen, **Boadicea**, led a series of successful rebellions against the Romans' occupation of England until she was eventually defeated in 62AD.

St Margaret's Church

She committed suicide and several places are claimed to be her last resting place, including the ground beneath *Kings Cross station*.

6 | THE CENOTAPH Whitehall SW1
Designed by Edwin Luytens in 1920, the monument is inscribed 'To the Glorious Dead'.

The nearest Sunday to Armistice Day (11th November) is known as Remembrance Sunday and a ceremony is held at the Cenotaph to remember all those who lost their lives in war.

The ceremony takes place between 10.30am and 11.30am, with a minute of silence respected throughout the country at 11.00am. The Queen and the royal dukes lay a wreath at the foot of the memorial.

WHITEHALL
On Whitehall stood the palace that was the administrative centre for the Tudor and Stuart monarchs. Today, most of the area is used by Government Ministries including those of Defence, Foreign Affairs, and the Treasury.

Whitehall Palace was originally called York Place and for over three centuries was the London home of the Archbishops of York.

When Cardinal Thomas Wolsey was Archbishop between 1514-1529 during the reign of **Henry VIII**, he extended York Place into a large and luxurious palace.

However, the king became increasingly resentful of Wolsey's power and wealth. And when the Cardinal failed to obtain from the Pope a quick conclusion for the divorce of Henry and Catherine of Aragon, he was dismissed.

With Wolsey gone, Henry moved into York Place and renamed it **WHITEHALL PALACE**. The name came from either its light stone or the custom of naming a place of pleasure a 'white hall'.

For Henry it was doubly attractive as a residence for at the time there were no apartments suitable for a queen. Catherine of Aragon was forced to live elsewhere, allowing Henry greater freedom in courting Anne Boleyn, his next wife.

Henry married Anne secretly at Whitehall in 1533. After her execution three years later, he married his third wife, Jane Seymour here.

Whitehall Palace covered twenty-four acres of river frontage and had two landing sites for the royal barge. The importance of being close to the Thames was that the river provided the fastest means of travel at the time.

From Whitehall, Henry VIII centralised the power of the monarchy and orchestrated the split from the Catholic Church in Rome. He created the Church of England with the sovereign at its head. During this Reformation, all monastic property was seized and the proceeds used to bolster the wealth of the monarchy.

THE BANQUETING HOUSE CORNER WHERE CHARLES I WAS EXECUTED

7 | BANQUETING HOUSE Whitehall SW1

Tel. (0171) 930 4179
Open Mon-Sat 10am-5pm
Admission charge

In 1603 **James I** came to the throne as the first monarch of both England and Scotland. As the first Stuart king, he decided to mark the new dynasty by rebuilding Whitehall as the greatest palace in Europe and he drew up plans to convert the two thousand-roomed building. However, time and money only allowed him to complete the Banqueting House. It was designed and built in 1622 by Inigo Jones, based on Italian Renaissance architecture.

The interior of the building was completed by **Charles I**. He chose Peter Paul Rubens to paint the ceiling. The highly political image shows James I deified and illustrates one of the central beliefs of the Stuart dynasty: the divine right of kings.

Charles believed this right gave him the authority to dissolve parliament and hold absolute power for nearly twenty years. However, the discontent led to the Civil War of the 1640s, ending in Charles's defeat.

EXECUTION OF A KING

On the freezing morning of 30th January 1649 Charles made his last walk from **St James's Palace** across **St James's Park** to the Banqueting House. And there, from under the gloriously painted ceiling, he stepped onto a balcony on the street for execution. He wore two thick undershirts to prevent shivering in front of the crowd. For Charles, as king, did not tremble at anything.

Oliver Cromwell, leader of the victorious Parliamentarian forces, became Lord Protector and lived in **Whitehall Palace** until his death there in 1658.

In 1660, **Charles II** made his triumphant return from exile in France. He made Whitehall the principal royal residence and began restoring the palace.

Charles took great pleasure in living in the great mass of rooms as he was able to keep his several mistresses and wife in separate areas.

The Duchess of Portsmouth was one mistress. As Louise de Keroualle she bore Charles a bastard son, given the title the Duke of Richmond. Ever difficult to please, her apartment was rebuilt three times before she was satisfied. **Diana, Princess of Wales**, is distantly related to Keroualle.

Several of the king's other mistresses are related to members of the present royal family: Princess Michael of Kent to Diane de Poitiers and **Sarah, Duchess of York**, to Lucy Walters.

Charles II died at Whitehall on 6th February 1685 from a urine infection caused by mercury poisoning.

His brother, **James II**, succeeded him but lived for only a short time at Whitehall.

A Roman Catholic, he was soon rejected by Protestant England and forced to flee Whitehall by river on 11th December 1688. During the king's escape the Great Seal of England was lost when it fell into the Thames.

The next monarchs **William and Mary** preferred the palaces at **St James's** and **Kensington**. As William suffered from asthma, he could not live near the river. Besides, the roads had improved and the comparative speed of river transport was no longer so great.

Whitehall Palace fell into decay.

On the 5th January 1698 a fire began in the laundry which destroyed most of the building. And for years it stood empty, surrounded by rubble.

Horse Guards THE CEREMONIAL ARCH

Eventually, in 1734, the government began to use the site again. The Treasury was the first building to go up, on the site of **Henry VIII's** original tennis courts.

Recently the wine cellars of the original palace have been excavated underneath the Ministry of Defence.

Today, only the Banqueting House remains of the palace at Whitehall.

8 | HORSE GUARDS Whitehall SW1
Changing the guard daily 11am
(Sun 10am)
Free

Horse Guards was built in 1751 on the site where the Stuart monarchs watched bear-baiting. The name comes from the Guards House of the original **Palace of Whitehall**.

The monarch travels through the arch from Horse Guards' Parade onto Whitehall for the State Opening of Parliament. Only the Sovereign is allowed to travel through the middle arch.

Horse Guards is home of the Household Cavalry, which guards the monarch.

9 | GREAT SCOTLAND YARD 4 Whitehall Place SW1
Private

On this site originally stood the house given to **Kenneth III** of Scotland by the English **Edgar** when he visited in 959AD. It was subsequently used by the Scottish Kings when attending the English Court.

Henry VIII's sister, Margaret, the widow of the Scottish **James IV**, was the last member of the Scottish royal family to live here.

Sometime after the Act of Union in 1707, the building was converted to offices and in 1829 became the first headquarters of the Metropolitan Police. The headquarters moved in 1890 to Millbank and then to *New Scotland Yard* in Victoria Street.

10 | STATUE OF CHARLES I Trafalgar Square WC2

The statue commemorates **Charles I**, executed in 1649.

Although Cromwell ordered the statue destroyed, it was buried and re-erected in 1660. Eight of those who had signed the death warrant of the king were executed here, facing the **Banqueting House**.

Every 30th January, on the anniversary of Charles's execution, a service is held by the statue and a wreath is laid at the **Banqueting House**.

It stands on the site of the original 'Charing Cross', pulled down in 1647. This was one of the crosses **Edward I** erected to commemorate the death of his wife, Eleanor of Castille. She died in Nottinghamshire in 1290 and each night where her body rested on its return to London, a cross was erected.

A replica cross stands outside nearby *Charing Cross Station*. The word 'Charing' comes from the French for 'dear Queen', 'Chere Reine'.

ST MARTIN-IN-
THE-FIELDS

11 | ST MARTIN-IN-THE-FIELDS St Martin's Place WC2
Tel. (0171) 930 0089
Free
Overlooking Trafalgar Square is the church where **Mary I** used to worship.
Charles II was christened here and his mistress, Nell Gwynne, buried. In the early eighteenth century, **George I** was a church warden.
   The present church was rebuilt in the eighteenth century and there is still a royal box to the left of the altar.

12 | NATIONAL GALLERY & NATIONAL PORTRAIT GALLERY
Trafalgar Square & 2 St Martin's Place WC2
Tel. National Gallery (0171) 839 3321
      National Portrait Gallery (0171) 306 0055
Open daily 10am-6pm (Sun 12-6pm)
Free
Some of the columns outside the National Gallery came from **George IV**'s
CARLTON HOUSE when it was demolished.
   Around the corner at the National Portrait Gallery, portraits of the monarchs of Great Britain are on display in the galleries and reveal much of the history and stories behind their reigns.

THE NATIONAL
GALLERY WITH
TRAFALGAR SQUARE

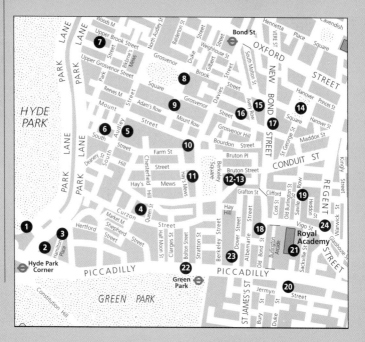

Piccadilly & Mayfair

QUEEN ELIZABETH
GATES THE ENTRANCE
TO HYDE PARK FROM
PARK LANE

1 | QUEEN ELIZABETH GATES Hyde Park SW1
Open daily 5am-dusk
Free
A recent addition to HYDE PARK, the Queen Elizabeth Gates honour **the Queen Mother** and mark the entrance of *Rotten Row* from Park Lane. (Rotten Row comes from 'rue de roi', French for King's Road.)

2 | INTER-CONTINENTAL HOTEL 145 Piccadilly W1
The hotel stands on the site of the 26 bedroom house where **George VI** lived prior to becoming king.
   Formerly he had lived at the **WHITE LODGE** in Richmond Park, but, preferring Central London, moved here in 1927.
   The house was destroyed by bombing during the Second World War.

3 | 5 HAMILTON PLACE W1
Private
Site of the former Les Ambassadeurs Club, a favourite night club of **Princess Margaret** in the 1960s.

4 | 6 QUEEN STREET W1
Private
Home to Louisa Fairbrother, the mistress of George, Duke of Cambridge.
   George was a cousin of **Queen Victoria** and wanted to marry Louisa, a commoner, who had borne him three sons. Victoria refused them permission and they never married.

5 | SOUTH AUDLEY STREET W1
Harry's Bar 26 South Audley Street
Favourite haunt of **Sarah**, **Duchess of York**, during her affair with Steve Wyatt.
Henry Maxwell 29 South Audley Street
Maker of the Queen's riding boots.
Purdey, James & Sons 57 South Audley Street
Suppliers of hunting guns to the royal family.

6 | 15 SOUTH STREET W1
Private

Home of Catherine Walter, the first mistress of the Prince of Wales (later **Edward VII**). They were lovers between 1867-1876.

7 | LE GAVROCHE 43 Upper Brook Street W1

Exclusive society restaurant and favourite of the royal circle.

> PUBLIC INFIDELITY
>
> Texan business man, Steve Wyatt, used Sarah Duchess of York's apartment in **BUCKINGHAM PALACE** for a secret and probably illegal meeting with an Iraqi oil executive.
>
> After the meeting they joined a party at Le Gavroche. At the infamous dinner, they were placed apart until Wyatt shouted loudly, "No one comes between me and my girl". To the shock of the other guests, he moved next to Sarah and they fondled each other throughout the rest of the meal.

8 | 7 GROSVENOR SQUARE W1
Private

At this address in 1919, the Duke of York (later **George VI**) met Lady Elizabeth Bowes-Lyon at a dinner party held by Lady Farquhar.

He proposed several months later at *St Paul's House*, the Bowes Lyon country home at Walden Bury, in Hertfordshire, where Elizabeth had been born.

9 | H R HIGGINS 79 Duke Street W1

Suppliers of coffee to the Queen.

10 | NICKY CLARKE 130 Mount Street W1

Hairdresser who styled and coloured **Diana**'s hair for many years. Her haircuts of the 1980s were copied all over the world.

11 | ANNABEL'S 44 Hays Mews W1
Private Club

Club established in the 1960s and named after Annabel Goldsmith, mother of Jemima Khan.

In July 1986 it was believed that **Prince Andrew** was to hold his stag night at the club. **Sarah**, accompanied by **Diana** and comedienne Pamela Stevenson, dressed as policewomen and attempted to crash the party. After finding he was not there, they left, embarrassed and pursued by the press.

12 | BERKELEY SQUARE HOUSE 17 Bruton Street W1
Private

Elizabeth II was born in a house on this site on 21st April 1926. The house was the London home of her grandparents, the Earl and Countess of Strathmore and was demolished in 1937.

13 | HOLLAND & HOLLAND 31 Bruton Street W1

The Duke of Edinburgh buys carriage equipment here. Since arthritis prevented him from riding, the duke has taken up the sport of carriage-riding.

14 | **VOGUE HOUSE** Hanover Square W1
Diana's sister used to work at the magazine.

Whilst visiting the offices before her wedding, Diana came upon dresses by David and Elizabeth Emanuel. She loved their work and asked them to design her wedding dress.

Diana visited Vogue House frequently for guidance on her new royal role. She received help in her dress, make-up and style by leading members of the magazine's fashion department. Vogue's fashion editor, Grace Coddington, taught Diana how to act in front of the cameras.

15 | **CLARIDGES HOTEL** Brook Street W1
The restaurant of this magnificent art-deco hotel is one of the most popular amongst today's royal family: **the Queen, the Queen Mother** and **Diana**, are all frequent diners.

Prince Charles has his hair cut by Richard Dalton, who works at Claridges Hairdressing.

Next door to Claridges is Edward Goodyear, florist to the royal family.

16 | **16 GROSVENOR STREET**
Private
Edward VIII's last mistress, Alice Keppel, lived here.

She had met Edward in 1898 and their affair continued until his death in 1910. Queen Alexandra allowed Alice to be present at his death-bed.

Camilla Parker-Bowles, mistress of **Prince Charles**, is a direct descendant of Alice Keppel.

17 | **NEW BOND STREET** W1
This street of exclusive shops has always catered for royalty and the aristocracy:
Fogal 36 New Bond Street
Here, Diana buys her hosiery and Charles his socks.
Asprey 165 New Bond Street
Jewellers used by the royal family.
Collingwood's 171 New Bond Street
This jewellers began its royal association in 1817 when the owner ran cockfights at the Horse & Groom at the top of *Brixton Hill* for the Prince Regent (later **George IV**). The pub was a convenient stop for the prince on his way to Brighton.
Cartier 175 New Bond Street
Royal jewellers who also sponsor Prince Charles's favourite sport, polo, at **Windsor Great Park**.

18 | **OLD BOND STREET** W1
The Embassy Club 6-8 Old Bond Street
Both **Edward VII** and **Edward VIII**, when Prince of Wales, had their own tables at this club. Established in the late nineteenth century, the club was known as the 400 Club just before its closure in 1920.

> **DUKE IN CLUB SCANDAL**
> **Edward VIII**'s brother, the Duke of Kent, a regular of the Embassy Club, frequented many other night-clubs and in the process developed a habit for cocaine. In the mid-1920s, he was arrested in a north London homosexual club. But the charges were dropped. The duke died in a plane crash in the 1940s after an all-night party.

Swaine, Adeney, Brigg & Sons 10A Old Bond Street
Suppliers of field sport equipment for the royal family. The shop has held a Royal Warrant since the eighteenth century when they made whips for George III.

19 | SAVILE ROW W1

The world's premier address for tailoring. Most male members of the royal family have suits made in this area.

Anderson & Sheppard 30 Savile Row
Prince Charles has recently begun having his suits made here. He prefers their double-breasted and loose cut jackets to disguise his wide hips. Charles likes his trousers to have turn-ups, a fashion first made famous by his great-uncle, Edward VIII, who saw them as a practical solution to the damp problems at Buckingham Palace.

Henry Poole & Co. 15 Savile Row
A traditional livery (uniform) tailor.
In the late nineteenth century, Poole & Co. made the uniforms for the Prince of Wales (later Edward VII): five for the British Honorary Orders; fifty for foreign Orders; and one for every regiment of the British Army.

Dege & Sons 10 Savile Row
Suppliers of ceremonial wear.

They made Queen Victoria's coronation robes in 1838. The present Queen and her mother still use them.

Bernard Weatherill 8 Savile Row
Another livery tailor holding three royal warrants. Weatherill used to be Speaker of the House of Commons.

Gieves & Hawkes 1 Savile Row
These famous tailors make the naval uniforms for the Duke of Edinburgh and the Prince of Wales. They have a strong tradition in this area of tailoring, as they made the clothes for Lord Nelson when he was Lord Admiral of the Fleet in the early nineteenth century.

GIEVES & HAWKES

Below Savile Row, at 16 Sackville Street, the Duke of Edinburgh buys his shirts and socks from Stephens Brothers.

20 | SHOPPING IN PICCADILLY W1

Simpsons 202 Piccadilly
  General supplier of clothing items to the royal family.
Hatchards 187 Piccadilly
  The Queen's favourite bookshop.
Fortnum & Mason 181 Piccadilly
This department store was established in 1707 by Charles Fortnum, a footman of George III.
Penhaligon 16 Burlington Arcade, Piccadilly
The Duke of Edinburgh buys his toiletries from this traditional perfumery.

21 | ROYAL ACADEMY OF ARTS ART SCHOOL Piccadilly W1
Private
Princess Margaret's daughter, Lady Sarah Chatto, completed her art training here. She studied initially at Camberwell College of Art on Peckham Road, south-east London.

22 | NAVAL & MILITARY CLUB 94 Piccadilly W1
Private
Once home to Adolphus, Duke of Cambridge, an uncle of **Queen Victoria**.
  On 27th May 1850, whilst visiting her uncle, Victoria was attacked in the courtyard by a Lieutenant Pate, retired from the 10th Hussars. He hit the queen over the head but she was not badly hurt and went on to the opera. Pate was arrested and later declared insane.
  Cambridge House became home to Lord Palmerston, one of Victoria's favourite Prime Ministers, from 1855-1865.

23 | CAPTAIN WATTS OF LONDON 5 Dover Street W1
The Duke of Edinburgh and Princess Anne buy their sailing clothes from the shop. They are both keen sailors and Princess Anne regularly spends her summers with husband Tim Lawrence on their small yacht cruising around the Scottish islands.

24 | REGENT STREET W1
Many of the buildings here stand on Crown land, including the Meridien Hotel, the Regent Palace Hotel and all of South Regent Street.
Café Royal 68 Regent Street
Frequent night spot of Edward VII.
Garrard & Co. 112 Regent Street
Jewellers who maintain the Crown Jewels at the Tower of London. They also make new additions to the collection.
  Garrard began as goldsmiths for William IV in the early nineteenth century. They made Queen Victoria's jubilee crown in 1870, which, because of her small frame, needed to be lighter than previous crowns.
  In 1981, to everyone's surprise, Prince Charles chose an engagement ring (costing £24,000) for Diana Spencer from Garrard's catalogue. Normally, the ring would have been specially made or have come from the Royal Collection.
Hamleys 188 Regent Street
Any toys purchased by the royal family are from this huge toy shop. Several floors display a magnificent range of children's playthings.

St Mary-le-Strand

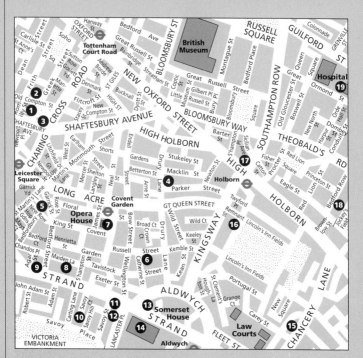

Soho, Covent Garden & Holborn

1 | KETTNERS 29 Romilly Street W1
One of the most fashionable restaurants in the early years of the twentieth century, when Edward VII would dine here with his various mistresses.

2 | WHEELER'S 19 Old Compton Street W1
This famous fish restaurant was where Prince Philip established a lunch club in the 1960s, where he would meet male friends every Thursday.

3 | PALACE THEATRE Shaftsbury Avenue W1

4 | NEW LONDON THEATRE Drury Lane WC2
After leaving the Royal Marines in 1988, **Prince Edward** worked as an assistant for the Really Useful Theatre Company.

Based at these two theatres for eighteen months, Edward worked on the productions of Andrew Lloyd Webber's Cats, Starlight Express, Aspects of Love and Phantom of the Opera in both London and New York.

He left in 1990 to join the unsuccessful Theatre Division.

5 | THE GARRICK CLUB 15 Garrick Street WC2
Private
A favourite male-only dining haunt of **Edward VII** and members of the Marlborough Circle.

6 | THEATRE ROYAL DRURY LANE Catherine Street WC2
A regular theatre destination for the royal family from the middle of the seventeenth century.

Charles II gave this theatre, along with the **OPERA HOUSE**, his royal patent in 1663.

Two years later, the king saw his future mistress, Nell Gwynne, making her stage debut at the Theatre in 'Indian Queen' by Dryden.

7 | ROYAL OPERA HOUSE Bow Street WC2
Opera has always been a favourite entertainment for the royal family, especially **Queen Victoria** who frequently came as a girl and **Princess Margaret** who also visits.

8 | RULES RESTAURANT 35 Maiden Lane WC2
Thomas Rule opened an oyster bar here in 1798.

The Prince of Wales (later Edward VII) ate at the restaurant when he visited the nearby Evan's Music Hall at 43 King Street.

9 | COUTTS & CO. 440 Strand WC2
The bank was established in 1692 and has held the household account of the monarch since George III in the 1760s.

Originally a goldsmith, Coutts established the royal connection when the bank sold silver plate to the Prince of Wales (later George II) in 1716.

All correspondence between the bank and **BUCKINGHAM PALACE** used to be taken by horse-drawn carriage until in 1993 security prevented it.

10 | THE SAVOY HOTEL Strand WC2

The Savoy Hotel stands on the site of the former Savoy Palace.

The palace was built in 1214 and leased by Peter of Savoy from his nephew, **Henry III**, for the token rent of three arrows a year.

It then passed into the family of the Duke of Lancaster and in 1361 was home to John of Gaunt, son of **Edward III**.

When **Richard II** ascended to the throne in 1377 aged only ten, it was his uncle, this duke, who wielded the power and made the decisions.

In 1381 the palace was destroyed during the Peasants' Revolt, when it was thought that the duke was behind the new heavy taxes.

The land forms part of the Duchy of Lancaster estate, which has been absorbed into the Crown. Queen's Chapel of the Savoy in a little square behind the hotel

11 | TWININGS 216 Strand WC2

Tea merchants who have supplied the royal family since Queen Victoria.

12 | THRESHER & GLENNY Lancaster Place WC2

Suppliers of evening wear to the royal family since 1783 when George III used them for his evening shirts.

13 | ST MARY-LE-STRAND Strand WC2

This church was where **George III** stationed the Chapel Royal.

The Chapel Royal is the spiritual department of the Royal Household. In earlier centuries, it would travel around the country with the monarch. For example in 1415, the choir sang in France for **Henry V** the night before the Battle of Agincourt.

Today, the Chapel Royal is based at **ST JAMES'S PALACE**.

14 | SOMERSET HOUSE Strand WC2

Access via Courtauld Institute Gallery
Tel. (0171) 873 2526
Open Mon-Sat 10am-6pm (Sun 2-6pm)
Admission charge

On the death of **Henry VIII**, his son **Edward VI** was the under-aged heir. The Duke of Somerset was made Lord Protector and immediately seized this land from the Bishops of Worcester and Chester to build a palace.

The duke instructed his workmen to take stones from **ST MARGARET'S CHURCH** in Westminster. However, the outrage was so great that armed guards were sent by Somerset's rivals to stop them.

In 1552, when Somerset was executed for treason the palace was left unfinished.

Eighty years later there was a need for more living space in the area. **Charles I** lived at **WHITEHALL PALACE** and his senior courtiers and noblemen filled the houses along the river. (The surrounding streets still carry their names: Southampton, Exeter, Essex, Burghley, Howard and Norfolk.) So, Somerset House was completed as apartments to house the over-spill of courtiers and guests.

Queen Henrietta, the wife of Charles I, used the building for extravagant entertainment and scandalised the growing Puritan movement by acting on the stage that she had built.

In 1658, nine years after he had executed **Charles I**, Oliver Cromwell died and lay in state at Somerset House for two months.

The monarchy was restored and the widowed Queen Henrietta returned from France to live at the house. Again it became a place of court festivities.

After **Charles II**'s death, his wife, Catherine of Braganza, moved in and introduced Italian opera to England.

George III's widow, Charlotte, was the last queen to live at Somerset House. But the house was in decay and she soon moved to Buckingham House.

15 | EDE & RAVENSCROFT 93 Chancery Lane WC2
Formal tailors who have made royal state robes for thirteen successive reigns.

THE QUEEN'S SOLICITORS **FARRER & CO.**

16 | FARRER & CO.
66 Lincoln's Inn Fields WC2
Solicitors to the royal family. The company was established in 1701 and is one of the oldest in the world.

In 1996, Fiona Shackleton represented **Prince Charles** during his divorce from **Diana**. As part of the settlement, Diana lost her HRH title but won a cash fund of £17 million and £500,000 annual income for life.

Sir Matthew Farrer represents **the Queen** and the trusts of her children.

17 | MISCHON DE REGA
21 Southampton Row WC1

Solicitor Anthony Julius represented **Diana** during her divorce from **Prince Charles**. For secrecy during the early divorce negotiations, Diana was known as Mrs Walsh.

18 | PRINCE'S TRUST HEADQUARTERS 8 Bedford Row WC1
The Trust was established in 1972 after George Pratt, a probation officer, asked **Charles** to help unemployed young people to set up their own businesses.

By 1977 the Trust was helping twelve thousand people through a network of a volunteers. And in 1994 the turnover was over £10 million.

19 | GREAT ORMOND STREET HOSPITAL WC1
Prince Charles had his appendix taken out here. This was the first time that a member of the immediate royal family had been admitted to hospital. Thirty years later his son **Prince William** was treated for a head injury, caused whilst playing golf at school.

NEVILLE HAIRDRESSERS

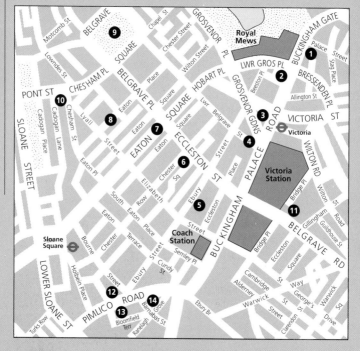

Belgravia

Belgravia is a grand residential area lying to the west of **BUCKINGHAM PALACE** and **WESTMINSTER**. Amongst the handful of shops and offices, many serve the royal family.

The area was once Ebury Farm, owned by **Edward I**. By 1676 it was owned by the Grosvenor family and named Belgravia after a village on their land in Leicestershire.

Thomas Cubitt developed the area before he was chosen by **Queen Victoria** to build Osborne House on the Isle of Wight in the 1840s.

Cubitt was made Lord Ashcombe. His family continues its royal connections through Camilla Parker Bowles, niece of the present Lord Ashcombe and mistress of **Prince Charles**. Indeed, when she first moved to London to work as a secretary, Camilla lived on the ground floor of Stack House on Ebury Street. *where she conducted her affair with charles in 1970's*

1 | THE DUCHY OF CORNWALL

10 Buckingham Gate SW1
Private

Offices of the Duchy of Cornwall, built in 1854 and distinguished by the Prince of Wales' feathers on the railings.

The Duchy of Cornwall was the first dukedom to be created in England. It was set up in the fourteenth century by **Edward III** to provide the Prince of Wales with an income.

The king's son, the first Duke of Cornwall, was known as the Black Prince. He lived in Kennington (Saxon for 'place of the king') and *Black Prince Road* marks the site of his palace.

ENTRANCE TO **THE DUCHY OF CORNWALL'S** OFFICES

Most of the Duchy's property is in the west of England, but amongst its London properties are the freehold of the *Oval Cricket Ground* and several streets in *Kennington* SE11.

Prince Charles, as heir to the throne, is the present Duke of Cornwall.

2 | J A ALLEN 1 Lower Grosvenor Place SW1

An equestrian bookshop from which the Queen buys books on horses. Racing and horse-breeding are her favourite interests.

3 | ANTHONY TATE 39 Grosvenor Gardens SW1

The chemist that serves Buckingham Palace.

4 | JOHN LIDSTONE'S 12 Belgrave Street SW1

The butcher serving Buckingham Palace.

5 | **HUGH & STEPHENS** 161 Ebury Road SW1

This hairdresser is used by Princess Michael of Kent.

6 | **CHESTER SQUARE** SW1
Private

Prince Andrew's first serious girlfriend was the American soft-porn actress, Koo Stark. She rented a basement flat in Chester Square at the time of their affair in the early 1980s. (No. 73 is home to Margaret Thatcher.)

7 | **EATON SQUARE** SW1
Private

Diana's grandmother, Lady Fermoy, lived in Eaton Square until her death in 1993.

Lady Fermoy was an old friend and lady-in-waiting to **the Queen Mother** and was instrumental in matchmaking the marriage of Diana and Prince Charles in 1981.

8 | **EATON PLACE** SW1
Private

Edward VII's most famous mistress, Lily Langtry, lived in an apartment in Eaton Place when she first moved to London from Jersey in 1876 with her husband, Edward Langtry.

Later, when she returned to London to begin a stage career, Lily lived at 18 Albert Mansions on Victoria Street. The mansion block has since been demolished.

9 | **INGESTRE HOUSE** 36 Belgrave Square SW1
Private

Queen Victoria's mother, the Duchess of Kent, moved to Ingestre House when Victoria became Queen. Victoria rented the house for £2,000 a year. Ingestre House was used until Clarence House became available on the death of Princess Augusta, the last surviving daughter of George III.

10 | **NEVILLE HAIRDRESSERS** 5 Pont Street SW1

The Queen has had her hair cut by Charles Martyn, of Neville Hairdressers, since 1968.

11 | **HOLIDAY INN HOTEL** 2 Bridge Place SW1

At midnight on 20th April 1990, **Prince Edward** met secretly with five other employees of Andrew Lloyd Webber's Really Useful Theatre Company. In a room on the 9th floor, of the then Scandic Crown Hotel, they agreed to resign and to set up their own company, Theatre Division.

The prince, preferring to be known as Edward Windsor, was made Technical Director. Unfortunately within a year the new company had folded.

After a period resting, Edward set up the television production company, **ARDENT PRODUCTIONS**.

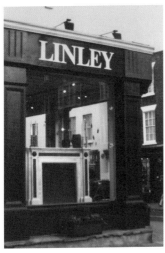

DAVID LINLEY'S SHOP AT **60 PIMLICO ROAD**

12 | 20 PIMLICO ROAD SW1
Private

In the early days of their relationship **Princess Margaret** secretly met with Anthony Armstrong-Jones at his combined flat and photographic studio. Armstrong-Jones had a motorbike and Margaret enjoyed the thrill of driving incognito around London.

Another secret meeting place was a friend's house overlooking the river, at *59 Rotherhithe Street*, south-east London, which has long since been demolished.

13 | 60 PIMLICO ROAD SW1

Princess Margaret's only son, David Linley, owns this shop.

Viscount Linley, who trained as a cabinet-maker, moved here from **1 NEW KING'S ROAD**.

14 | 110 PIMLICO ROAD SW1

La Fontana restaurant has been a regular lunch-time place for Diana and her sister, Lady Jane Fellowes. Her favourite dish is mozzarella and tomato salad.

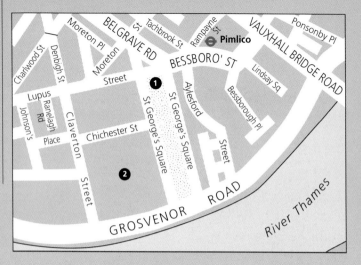

Pimlico

Pimlico is named after an ancient Saxon manor, lying between **BELGRAVIA** and the river Thames. Its connections with the royal family are recent.

DIANA
PHOTOGRAPHED AT
ST SAVIOUR'S HALL
SHORTLY BEFORE HER
ENGAGEMENT TO
PRINCE CHARLES

1 | ST SAVIOUR'S HALL St George's Square SW1
Private
Diana was working as a nursery school assistant at the Young England Kindergarten in 1980 when **Prince Charles** began his courtship.

The garden behind the hall was the location for the famous photograph of 'Lady Di' wearing a see-through skirt and carrying a child on her hip.

2 | DOLPHIN SQUARE SW1
Private
The Queen's only daughter, **Princess Anne**, lives in a flat in Dolphin Square with her second husband, Commander Timothy Lawrence. The couple married on 12th December 1992 in a quiet ceremony. They chose the square because it is both informal and private.

The complex of 1,250 flats overlooking the river was built in 1937 and at that time was the largest block of apartments in Europe.

Anne was made Princess Royal in 1987. This was both in recognition of her charity work and to distinguish her from the two new royal Princesses, Diana and Sarah. In October 1996, the Queen honoured Anne further by making her a member of the Scottish Royal Order of the Thistle.

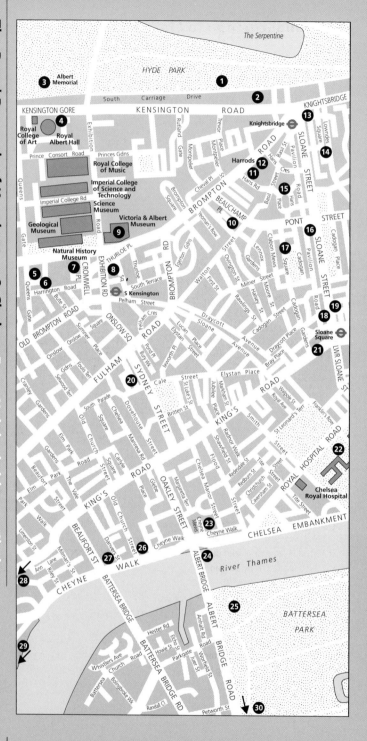

The Serpentine

HYDE PARK

3 Albert Memorial

South Carriage Drive

KENSINGTON ROAD

1

2

KNIGHTSBRIDGE

13

Knightsbridge

KENSINGTON GORE

Royal College of Art

4 Royal Albert Hall

Prince Consort Road

Princes Gdns

Prince Consort Road

Royal College of Music

Imperial College of Science and Technology

Imperial College Rd

Science Museum

Geological Museum

Victoria & Albert Museum **9**

Natural History Museum **7**

Lowndes Square

14

SLOANE STREET

Harrods **12**

11

Pavilion Road

Basil St

Hans Cres

Hans Rd

15

Basil Street

Hans Place

BEAUCHAMP PL

BROMPTON RD

10

PONT STREET

16

Cadogan Place

SLOANE STREET

17

Lennox Gardens

Clabon Mews

Pavilion Road

Cadogan

5

6

Harrington Road

EXHIBITION PL

CROMWELL

8

THURLOE PL

Thurloe Sq

Thurloe Square

S Kensington

South Terrace

Pelham Street

Queens Gate

OLD BROMPTON ROAD

Cranley Gardens

Onslow Gardens

Onslow

Sumner Place

Selwood Terr

Fulham Road

ONSLOW SQ

Pelham Cres

Pond Pl

Lucan Pl

Ixworth Pl

Elystan Pl

Bury St

Pelham Street

Draycott

Walton Street

Ovington St

First St

Milner Street

Moore Street

Halsey St

Rawlings St

Cadogan Street

Cadogan Gardens

Draycott Place

18

19

Sloane Square

21

Sloane Avenue

Draycott Avenue

SYDNEY STREET

20

FULHAM ROAD

South Parade

Old Church Street

Chelsea Square

Dovehouse Street

Cale Street

Britten St

St Luke's St

Jubilee Place

Markham St

St Luke's St

Elystan Place

KING'S

ROAD

Smith

Royal Ave

Wellington Sq

Anderson St

St Leonard's Terr

Franklin's Row

LWR SLOANE ST

ROYAL HOSPITAL ROAD

22

Chelsea Royal Hospital

Tite Street

BEAUFORT ST

Elm Park Gardens

Beaufort Gardens

The Vale

Elm Park Road

KING'S

ROAD

Carlyle Square

Oakley Street

OAKLEY STREET

Manresa Rd

Glebe Place

Margaretta Terr

Flood Street

Shawfield St

Redesdale St

Radnor Walk

Redburn St

Christchurch St

Tedworth Sq

Caversham St

Chelsea Manor Street

Tite Street

Ralston St

23

Cheyne Mews

Cheyne Walk

CHELSEA EMBANKMENT

26

27

Danvers St

CHEYNE WALK

28

Ann Lane

Milman's St

Riley St

CHEYNE

BATTERSEA BRIDGE

24

ALBERT BRIDGE

River Thames

25

BATTERSEA PARK

29

Whistlers Ave

Battersea Church Road

Bolingbroke Wlk

Hester Rd

Howie St

Parkgate Road

Echo St

Anhalt Rd

Worfield St

Juer St

ALBERT BRIDGE ROAD

BATTERSEA BRIDGE RD

Randall Cl

Petworth St

30

From Knightsbridge to Chelsea

The area has a long association with the monarchy and was made 'Royal' in 1901 to commemorate it as the birthplace of **Queen Victoria**.

The borough is made up of several ancient villages: **Chelsea** (Saxon for 'shelf of sand'), **Kensington** (Anglo-Saxon for 'Cynesige's Farm') and **Knightsbridge** (named after the bridge over the River Westbourne at Kensington Gore, where traditionally knights fought duels)

HYDE PARK VIEW OF THE SERPENTINE LAKE

1 | HYDE PARK SW1

Tel. (0171) 298 2100

Open daily 5am-midnight

Free

The 340 acres of Hyde Park are royal land through which the Westbourne River runs, from Hampstead via the Serpentine Lake to the Thames. 'Hyde' comes from the Saxon word meaning 'a hundred acres'.

Up to 1536, the area belonged to St Peter's of Westminster (**WESTMINSTER ABBEY**) and was forest where deer, boar and wild bull roamed.

Hyde Park became royal land during the Reformation when **Henry VIII** took possession and used it for hunting.

James I opened the park to the public as a fashionable place of entertainment. During the Civil War of the 1640s, the Parliamentary Forces fortified the park near Park Lane against the Royalists.

With the monarchy's restoration in 1660, Hyde Park was again given over to popular entertainment and **Charles II** would frequently come to the park to view fashionable society promenading before him.

The execution site of Tyburn Tree stands on the present *Speakers' Corner in the north-east of the park*. Named after another local river, it was a site of hanging from the twelfth to the eighteenth century.

In 1571, the original tree was replaced with a triangular mass of wooden poles. It stood twelve feet high and was able to hang up to eight people at any one time.

Queen Victoria allowed the use of Hyde Park for the *1851 Great Exhibition*. The huge glass exhibition hall was situated by Rutland Gate. The exhibition was a great success and Albert, as head of the organising committee, was soon awarded the title of Prince Consort.

After the exhibition, the hall was moved to a specially built park in south London, which was renamed Crystal Palace. It burnt down in 1936.

2 | KNIGHTSBRIDGE BARRACKS Knightsbridge SW7
Private

These barracks were built in 1959 for the Household Cavalry. The grandest aristocratic families traditionally make up members of this regiment.

The Changing of the Guard begins here when the new guard ride on horseback along the edge of the park towards **BUCKINGHAM PALACE**.

THE ROYAL ALBERT HALL A MONUMENT DEDICATED TO THE MEMORY OF PRINCE ALBERT

3 | ALBERT MEMORIAL Kensington Gardens SW7
Queen Victoria chose George Gilbert Scott to design the monument to the Prince Consort. The statue portrays Albert reading from a catalogue of the 1851 Great Exhibition, his greatest achievement.

4 | ROYAL ALBERT HALL Kensington Gore SW7
Tel. (0171) 589 3203

The Royal Albert Hall, another monument to Victoria's late husband, was completed in July 1872 and opened by the Prince of Wales (later **Edward VII**) after **Queen Victoria** was too upset to attend.

The project had begun three years after **Albert's death** in May 1864 but was stopped twice through lack of funds.

The concert hall originally had a notorious echo and it was said to be the *one* place a composer could hear his work played twice.

5 | QUEEN'S GATE SCHOOL 131 Queen's Gate SW7
Private
Prince Charles's mistress, Camilla Parker-Bowles, went to this nursery school in 1957.

6 | PINEAPPLE DANCE STUDIOS
38 Harrington Road SW7
Diana, Princess of Wales, had dance lessons here, when it was the Vacani School and later when it became the Pineapple Dance Studios.

In the late 1970s, Diana spent three months training to become a dance teacher.

As Princess of Wales, she returned for private ballet and tap lessons, until she was recognised. Then the teachers came to her, at **BUCKINGHAM PALACE**.

Diana also took lessons at the *Royal Ballet School* at 155 Talgarth Road in West Kensington, after the birth of her second son, Prince Harry.

After these lessons in December 1985, she famously danced with Wayne Sleep at the **ROYAL OPERA HOUSE**.

7 | MILLAIS' HOUSE 7 Cromwell Place SW7
Private
The Victorian painter, John Everett Millais, painted a portrait of Lily Langtry in his studio in this building. When the Prince of Wales (later **Edward VII**) visited the studio, he was so attracted to the portrait that he insisted on being introduced. And soon Lily Langtry became his mistress.

8 | HEADLINES 33 Thurloe Place SW7
The beauty salon Diana uses for wax treatments.

9 | VICTORIA & ALBERT MUSEUM Cromwell Road SW7
Tel. (0171) 938 8500
Open Tue-Sun 10.00am-5.50pm (Mon 12.00-5.50pm)
Admission charge
Prince Albert suggested that profits from the 1851 Great Exhibition be used to develop a site of museums, schools and colleges. A farm at Kensington Gore was acquired for this purpose.

The first museum to open was the Victoria and Albert on 26th June 1909.

Many road names and buildings in the area are named after the prince: the Royal Albert Hall, Prince Consort Road, Prince's Gardens.

KNIGHTBRIDGE SHOPPING
10 | Beauchamp Place
The favourite shopping and dining street for **Diana, Princess of Wales**:
San Lorenzo, her favourite restaurant, is owned by a close friend
Beauchamp Foot and Body Care at no.48 where Diana comes for various treatments including colonic irrigation

Janet Reger's underwear shop
John Boyd, the hatter
Bruce Oldfield, dress designer
The Kanga Boutique at no.8, owned by designer Lady Tyron, a close friend of Prince Charles

11 | **Rigby and Peller** 2 Hans Road SW3
Virtually next door to Harrods is the exclusive lingerie shop where members of the royal family buy their underwear.

12 | **Harrods** Old Brompton Road SW3
Harrods supplies a range of produce to Buckingham Palace. Members of the royal family buy Christmas presents here, when the shop is closed to the public.

The Duke of Edinburgh and the Prince of Wales make frequent purchases from the Man's Shop, on the ground floor. And the Queen Mother buys her china and glass here.

13 | **Harvey Nichols** Knightsbridge SW1
This is Diana's favourite department store and she can often be seen here.

Immediately after their divorce, Prince Charles instructed the store not to send him any more of Diana's bills.

HILL HOUSE SCHOOL

14 | **19 LOWNDES SQUARE** SW1
Private
In the 1950s, **Princess Margaret** used the home of the Marquess of Abergavenny to meet her divorced lover, Peter Townshend.

15 | **HILL HOUSE SCHOOL**
17 Hans Place SW1
Private
When **Prince Charles** was sent to this preparatory school in 1956, he became the first member of the royal family to attend a school.

The shy prince was at first unhappy and missed the nannies who had brought him up at Buckingham Palace. However whilst at Hill House, he learnt to enjoy art, history and French, even if he hated the outdoor games played at the Duke of York's barracks on the King's Road SW3.

The pupils walk between the school's several locations in the distinctive uniform of short brown trousers.

16 | **CADOGAN HOTEL** Sloane Street SW1
Lily Langtry lived at 21 Pont Street after ending her affair with **Edward VII**.

The house is now incorporated into the Cadogan Hotel, with her drawing room as the Langtry Room.

17 | 34 CADOGAN SQUARE SW1
Private
Steve Wyatt, a Texas millionaire, lived here at the time of his affair with **Sarah, Duchess of York**. Intimate photographs of the couple were found in the flat, which hastened the break-up of the Duchess's marriage.

Chelsea was also home to another of the Duchess's American friends, her 'financial adviser' John Bryant.

SHOPPING IN CHELSEA:
18 | General Trading Company 144 Sloane Street SW1
Here, the royal family purchase smaller gifts.

19 | Moyses Stevens 157 Sloane Street SW1
This florist, established in 1872, supplies flowers and floral decorations for the Queen Mother at Clarence House.

20 | Catherine Walker 65 Sydney Street SW3
The British dress designer used by Diana.

21 | KING'S ROAD
Charles II built this private road in the seventeenth century to run from St James's Palace to Hampton Court.

It was only opened to the public in 1830.

Chelsea Royal Hospital

22 | CHELSEA ROYAL HOSPITAL Royal Hospital Road SW3
Tel. (0171) 730 0161
Open Mon-Sat 10-12am & 2-4pm (April-Sept: also Sun 2-4pm)
Free
Charles II commissioned the Royal Hospital to be built in 1682 by Christopher Wren as a home for pensioned soldiers.

Before losing his throne, Charles's brother, **James II,** had intended to use the building as part of a new palace.

Each June, the red-coated veterans commemorate their founder, Charles II, when they place oak branches around his statue in the grounds of the hospital. This refers to Charles fleeing during the Civil War and hiding in an oak tree at Boscobel Wood after the **BATTLE OF WORCESTER**.

23 | **CHEYNE MEWS** off Cheyne Walk SW3
In 1536, **Henry VIII** built a manor house on the site of the present Cheyne Mews.

The king gave the house to his last wife, Katherine Parr in 1543 as a wedding present and she retired after his death remaining here until her own.

In 1548, the house was given to the Duke of Northumberland, the Lord Protector of **Edward VI**.

Chelsea Manor House was demolished in the eighteenth century. Nearby Chelsea Manor Street was named after the house.

24 | **ALBERT BRIDGE** Chelsea Embankment SW3
The bridge was built in 1873 and, along with the *Albert Embankment*, was dedicated to Prince Albert.

Albert Bridge was built towards the end of **Queen Victoria**'s years of mourning. During the peak of her grief, the queen let it be known that she would knight the mayor of any city who erected a statue or memorial to her husband.

25 | **BATTERSEA PARK** Albert Bridge Road SW11
Tel. (0181) 871 7530
Open daily 5am-dusk
Free

Charles II frequently swam in pools created from the marshland of this area. In 1671 it was the site of a failed assassination attempt by Colonel Blood on the king.

Blood is most notorious for his later attempt to steal the Crown Jewels. Though he did manage to break into the **TOWER OF LONDON**, he was caught whilst leaving with the jewels. He refused to speak to anyone but the king, and to everyone's amazement, **Charles II** pardoned him. In fact Blood so charmed the king that he was awarded estates in Ireland and a pension of £500 a year.

Prince of Wales Drive, which borders the south side of the park, and its many blocks of flats are named after **Edward VII**.

Battersea Park, created in the 1890s, was financed by the selling of adjoining land for the construction of the mansion flats.

26 | **CHELSEA OLD CHURCH** Cheyne Walk SW3
Tel. (0171) 352 5627
Henry VIII is thought to have married his third wife, Jane Seymour, at this church in private before the state ceremony.

Originally built in 1157, the church suffered severe bomb-damage during the Second World War.

27 | CROSBY HALL Cheyne Walk SW10
Private

In 1483 Richard of Gloucester (later **Richard III**) was living in the hall when he was pronounced King, after **Edward V** had been murdered.

Crosby Hall was moved here in the early twentieth century from its original site in the City and now stands in the old garden of Thomas Moore's house. Moore was **Henry VIII**'s friend and chancellor before being executed for refusing to acknowledge the king as head of the reformed Church of England.

28 | 1 NEW KING'S ROAD SW10

This was the first shop of the Queen's nephew, David Linley, after training as a cabinet-maker. The shop has moved to a more prestigious location at **60 PIMLICO ROAD**.

29 | DEALS RESTAURANT Chelsea Harbour SW10

Two of the Queen's relatives own this restaurant: her nephew David Linley and her cousin Patrick Litchfield.

The name Deals comes from their initials: **D**avid Linley, **E**ddie Limm (the chef) **A**nd Patrick **L**itchfield'**S**.

30 | BATTERSEA
Old School House Este Road SW11
Private

David Linley and his wife, Serena Stanhope, live in the 4,000sq.ft penthouse flat.

40 Lavender Gardens SW11
Private

Sarah Ferguson rented this flat when she worked in public relations at the time of her engagement to **Prince Andrew**.

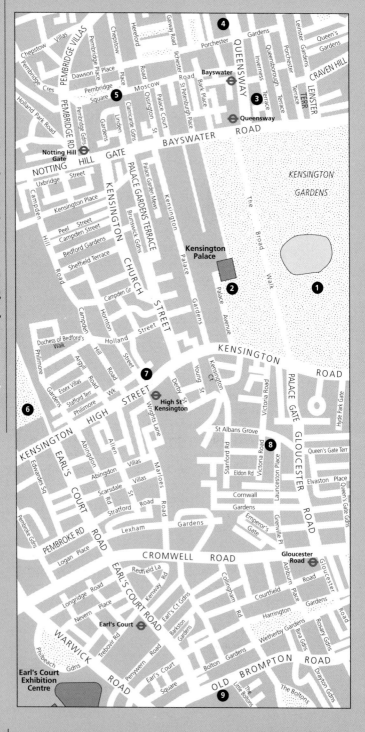

Kensington

KENSINGTON GARDENS LOOKING TOWARDS THE PALACE

1 | KENSINGTON GARDENS W8
Tel. (0171) 724 2826
Open daily 5am-dusk
Free
Kensington Gardens originally formed part of the **HYDE PARK** hunting forest.

It became gardens when **Queen Anne** enclosed a hundred acres to add to the twenty-six acres of garden already at 'Kensington House'. She built an Orangery and used the rest as a deer park.

Queen Caroline (wife of **George II**) further improved the gardens in the 1720s when she dammed the river Westbourne to create the Serpentine lake and the Round Pond. She kept two pleasure yachts on the lake. Later, a further three hundred acres of **HYDE PARK** were enclosed for her collection of exotic animals. The gardens were semi-public places for the king and queen to walk.

ROYAL ROBBERY
William IV told the story of how his great-grandfather, **George II,** was robbed on one such walk.

The king was approached by a man who, with great respect, told him that poverty forced him to steal. He demanded the king's possessions, including his watch and chain, jewellery and shoe buckle.

George gave the objects to the man, but asked if he could keep the seal attached to the watch chain, as it was only of sentimental value. The man agreed to return the seal the next day, providing the king said nothing of the robbery. The robber was true to his word and the king was given back the Royal Seal.

On the death of **George II**, Kensington Gardens were opened permanently to the public.

KENSINGTON PALACE
THE PRIVATE APARTMENTS

2 | KENSINGTON PALACE W8

Tel. (0171) 937 9561
Open daily 9am-5pm (Sun 11am-5pm)
Admission charge

THE HISTORY

William and Mary bought Nottingham House, a Jacobean mansion, as a winter residence. In June 1689 they renamed it Kensington House and commissioned their favourite architects, Christopher Wren and Nicholas Hawksmoor, to redesign the building.

While the early work was in progress, they stayed at **HOLLAND HOUSE**, until December 1689, when they moved in.

As they were joint monarchs, everything had to be built in twos: two sets of private apartments, two formal staircases. However as Kensington House was their private home, it was not constructed in a grand manner. The main changes were to increase the space: additional corner pavilions and a new south front; accommodation for the court entourage; and a private road to Hyde Park Corner. This road, now *South Carriage Drive*, was a frequent target for highwaymen until it became the first road in England to be lit by lamps.

Kensington House was Mary's favourite home. However she only enjoyed it for a few years, as she died here of smallpox in December 1694. Her husband followed eight years later in 1702 after falling from his horse.

When **Anne** became Queen, she moved from nearby Campden House. She had lived there for five years prior to her accession, with her only surviving child, the Duke of Gloucester. The house was demolished in 1900.

At Kensington House, she lived in the apartments built for her sister, Mary. Anne had hated William when alive and could not bear to use his rooms even after his death.

During her reign, Kensington House began to change from a country retreat to the centre of a fashionable area.

Anne spent much time at Kensington with her close friend, Sarah, the Duchess of Marlborough. They lived in intimate domesticity, calling each other Mrs Morley and Mrs Freeman.

Anne died after a stroke at Kensington House in 1714.

Her husband, Prince George of Denmark, had spent much of his time at his house on *Denmark Hill*, south London where the surrounding forest and marshland provided excellent hunting. Nearby *Dog Kennel Hill* was named after the stables, where he kept his dogs.

George I and **George II** transformed the house into Kensington Palace when in the 1720s the State Apartments were added.

George II was the last monarch to live at Kensington Palace. He died here in 1760.

After his death the palace was split into separate apartments for family members as future monarchs preferred St James's Palace or the newly purchased Buckingham House.

CHILDHOOD HOME OF VICTORIA

Queen Victoria was born on 24th May 1819 in the north-east ground-floor apartment.

Her father, the Duke of Kent, was the younger brother of **William IV**. As the king had no children, his brothers raced to produce an heir to the throne. The duke married Victoria of Saxe-Coburg, the widow of Prince Emich of Leningen. She was soon pregnant and the new-born baby was baptised Alexandrina Victoria in the Cupola Room at the palace. A few months later, the duke died.

Victoria led a sheltered and lonely childhood at Kensington Palace. Throughout her youth she shared a room with her mother and only when she became queen was she able to have her own room.

Victoria had very few companions other than her mother and Baroness Lehzen, her governess. Her days were spent in lessons, broken by a daily ride and the occasional visit to the opera at Covent Garden.

Victoria's life changed on 18th May 1836 when her German cousin, Prince Albert of Saxe-Coburg-Gotha, visited. She fell in love immediately and corresponded daily until proposing to Albert four years later.

Victoria became queen on 20th June 1837, when she was awoken to be told that her uncle had died. In the early morning she held her first Privy Council meeting in the Red Salon of the palace.

As queen, she made Buckingham Palace her official residence. However she opened the state apartments of Kensington to the public in 1898 after saving the palace from demolition by obtaining a parliamentary grant for its restoration.

The last queen to be born at Kensington Palace was Princess May of Teck in 1867. Born into the same apartments as Queen Victoria, the princess became known as **Queen Mary** (wife of **George V**).

THE TWENTIETH CENTURY: THE PRIVATE APARTMENTS

■ **Diana, Princess of Wales**, has apartment No. 8 where she has lived alone since her divorce from **Prince Charles**. During their marriage they lived in both Nos. 8 and 9, a large three-storied, L-shaped series of rooms.

■ **Prince Michael of Kent**, cousin of the Queen, lives at No.10, in Princess Margaret's old apartment.

■ **Princess Margaret** moved in 1963 to No. 1A Clock Court, a much larger apartment with twenty-one rooms over four storeys.

Margaret owns *Les Jolie Eaux* at Gelliceaux Bay on the island of Mustique. The villa was given as a wedding present to Margaret by the owner of Mustique, Colin Tennant. She visits every February.

   She spends summer in Turkey and Italy, September at **BALMORAL** and Christmas at **SANDRINGHAM**. Weekends are at the **ROYAL LODGE, WINDSOR** with the Queen Mother, or with friends, such as Earl Delaware, at Withyam in East Sussex.

Her two children, Sarah and David, were born and brought up in Kensington Palace.

   Sarah is an artist and has a studio in her house off *Kensington Church Street*.

   David, Viscount Linley, went to Gibbs School in Kensington with his cousins Prince Andrew and Prince Edward. He then went to **ASHDOWN HOUSE SCHOOL** in Sussex when he was eight years old, before going to *Bedales* in south-west England with his sister.

■ **The Duke of Gloucester**, a cousin of the Queen, also has a large apartment in the complex.

■ **Sir Robert Fellowes** lived in the *Old Barracks* when he was Private Secretary to the Queen. He resigned in summer 1996. His wife is Lady Jane Fellowes, a sister of Diana.

3 | INVERNESS COURT HOTEL 1 Inverness Terrace W2

Edward VII bought his mistress Lily Langtry a townhouse on the site of the Inverness Court Hotel. The house was only a short carriage-ride from his home at **MARLBOROUGH HOUSE** and convenient for their meetings.

4 | WHITELEYS OF BAYSWATER Queensway W2

Whiteleys was the first fashionable department store in London.

   It was a favourite of **Queen Mary** who during the 1920s made her purchases sweeping through the aisles in a heavy dress, waving a long-handled umbrella.

5 | WETHERBY SCHOOL 11 Pembridge Square W2
Private

Prince William's first school. His younger brother **Prince Harry** also attended after a private nursery school in nearby *Chepstow Villas*.

   William was named 'Basher Wills' after thumping another child in his first week. Lord Freddie Windsor, son of Prince Michael of Kent, also attends the school.

6 | HOLLAND HOUSE Holland Park, Ilchester Place W8
Tel. (0171) 602 9438
Open daily 8am-7pm (Oct-March: daily 8am-5pm)
Free

William and Mary lived in the Jacobean mansion for three months to be near the building works going on at **KENSINGTON PALACE**.

Holland House NOW A RESTAURANT AND HOSTEL IN HOLLAND PARK

7 | McDONALDS 108 Kensington High Street W8
Diana occasionally takes her sons here for a treat.

In June 1991 she brought Prince William here after treatment for a minor head injury at **Great Ormond Street Hospital**.

8 | LAUNCESTON PLACE 1A Launceston Place W8
A restaurant where **Diana** regularly meets friends for lunch.

Coleherne Court
Diana's London
home before
marriage to Charles

9 | 60 COLEHERNE COURT Old Brompton Road SW5
Private
Diana bought a ground-floor flat in Block H when she came to London.

Diana worked in various jobs including cleaning friend's flats and as a nursery assistant in Pimlico. She lived here with three flatmates during her engagement to **Prince Charles**.

One flatmate, Caroline Bartholomew, helped Andrew Morton with his biography, 'Diana Her Own Story'. Caroline is godmother to Prince Harry.

In spring 1997, Prince Edward's girlfriend of several years, Sophie Rhys-Jones, moved into a flat in Coleherne Court

CHESTER TERRACE

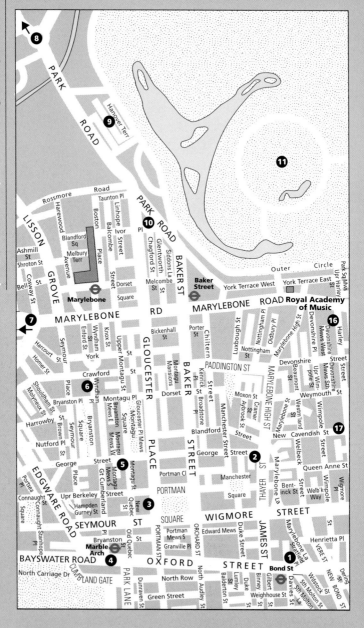

PARK ROAD

❽

❾ Hanover Terr

❶❶

Rossmore Road

Taunton Pl

LISSON GROVE

Harewood

Linhope St

Boston Place

Ivor

Balcombe Street

Blandford Sq

Chagford St

Glentworth St

PARK ROAD

❿ Pl

BAKER ST

Siddons La

Melcombe St

Ashmill St

Shroton St

Melbury Terr

Dorset Square

Bell St

Cosway St

Marylebone

Baker Street

York Terrace West

Outer Circle

Park Sq Mws

Upr Harley St

York Terrace East

St

MARYLEBONE

ROAD Royal Academy of Music

❼

MARYLEBONE

RD

Bickenhall St

Porter St

Chiltern St

Nottingham Pl

Luxborough St

Marylebone High St

Devonshire St

Devonshire Mews West

Devonshire Mews Sth

Harley

Street

❶❻

Harcourt St

Seymour Pl

Wyndham St

Knox St

York St

Enford St

Upper Montagu St

GLOUCESTER PLACE

Montagu Mansions

Dorset St

PADDINGTON ST

Manchester Street

Baker Street

Paddington St

Kenrick Pl

Aybrook St

Broadstone

Moxon St

Cramer St

Marylebone La

Beaumont St

Upr Wimpole St

Devonshire

Weymouth St

Wimpole

Street

❶❼

Homer St

Crawford Place

❻ Wyndham Pl

Montagu Sq

Gloucester Pl Mews

Montagu Mews E

Montagu Mews W

Blandford Street

Westmoreland St

New Cavendish St

Welbeck Street

Shouldham St

Molyneux St

Bryanston Pl

Montagu St

St

Harrowby St

Brown St

Seymour St

Bryanston Square

George Street

George Street

Manchester

Square

Queen Anne St

Welb'k Way

Wigmore Pl

Nutford Pl

EDGWARE ROAD

❺ Montagu Mews S

Gt Cumberland Pl

Montagu St

New Quebec St

Portman Cl

PORTMAN SQUARE

WIGMORE STREET

Bentinck St

JAMES ST

Wigmore St

Portsea Pl

Connaught Pl

Stanhope Pl

Upr Berkeley St

❸ Hampden Gurney St

Old Quebec St

SEYMOUR ST

PORTMAN ST

ORCHARD ST

Edward Mews

Duke Street

Henrietta Pl

Marylebone La

Stratford Pl

❶ Bond St

Connaught Square

Bryanston St

❹ Marble Arch

OXFORD

STREET

Portman Mews S

Granville Pl

North Row

Lumley St

Binney St

Gilbert St

Weighhouse St

Duke St

NEW BOND ST

Sth Molton La

Davies St

Davies St

Woodstock St

Dering St

BAYSWATER ROAD

North Carriage Dr

CUMBERLAND GATE

PARK LANE

Dunraven St

Green Street

North Audley St

Balderton St

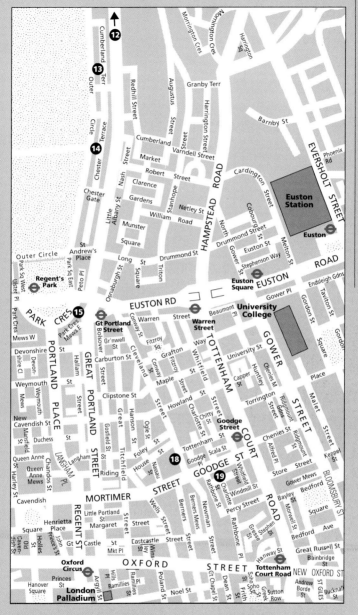

Around Regent's Park

Like Regent Street, much of Oxford Street stands on Crown Land. Among the many sites in the area with royal connections are:

1 | STRATFORD PLACE W1
Private
The Prince of Wales (later **Edward VII**) had been attracted to a portrait of Lily Langtry he had seen at **MILLAIS'S STUDIO** in South Kensington. And it was here at the home of a mutual friend, Sir Allen Young, that they were introduced. Soon after this meeting, she became his mistress.

2 | JOHNS & PEGG 11 George Street W1
Prince Charles has his ceremonial uniforms made by these military tailors.

3 | CHURCHILL HOTEL 30 Portman Square W1
Edward VII's last mistress, Alice Keppel, lived in a house on this site when they began their affair.

MARBLE ARCH

4 | MARBLE ARCH W1
The architect John Nash based Marble Arch on Constantine's Arch in Rome. It was first placed outside **BUCKINGHAM PALACE** as **George IV**'s grand entrance from the Mall.

Built as part of the king's redevelopment of the palace, the arch commemorated the two great victories of Trafalgar and Waterloo.

Unfortunately it was too narrow for the State Coach to pass through and so **Queen Victoria** moved Marble Arch to its present site.

5 | BRYANSTON COURT George Street W1
Wallis and Ernest Simpson lived in an apartment in Bryanston Court when they first moved from the United States to London.

Wallis Simpson won the Prince of Wales (later **Edward VIII**) in 1929 from another American, Thelma Morgan Furness.

6 | 15 WYNDHAM PLACE W1
Diana visits beautician Janet Filderman for her manicures and facials.

7 | ST MARY'S HOSPITAL PADDINGTON Praed Street W2
Here on 20th June 1982, **Diana** gave birth to Prince William. It was the first time that a future heir to the throne had been born in a hospital.
Diana used private rooms on the top floor of the Lindo Wing with three rooms either side cleared to provide the princess with a bathroom.

8 | HUMANA WELLINGTON HOSPITAL 8A Wellington Road NW8
Diana's father, Earl Spencer, died here after a heart attack in 1992.

9 | 7 HANOVER TERRACE NW1
Private
After Wallis Simpson had begun her affair with the Prince of Wales (later **Edward VIII**) she moved her with her husband Ernest.

10 | FRANCIS HOLLAND SCHOOL Ivor Place NW1
Private
Princess Margaret's daughter, Sarah Armstrong-Jones, went to this preparatory school.

REGENTS PARK THE BAND PAVILION

11 | REGENTS PARK NW1
Tel. (0171) 486 7905
Open daily 5am-dusk
Free
The Crown owns Regent's Park and eight hundred buildings on its perimeter.
Originally known as Marylebone Park Fields, it was part of a larger hunting forest belonging to **Henry VIII**.

Elizabeth I had a hunting lodge opposite *York Gate* where in 1600 she entertained the Emperor of Russia. The lodge was demolished in 1791.

In 1646 **Charles I** used the land to raise money during the Civil War. And after his execution the Commonwealth further reduced the forest by using the trees for naval construction.

When **Charles II** was restored as king, the land was leased as farmland to various noblemen.

The leases expired in 1811 and the Prince Regent (later **George IV**) decided to use the land for building expensive housing.

After several false starts John Nash was engaged in 1812 to design the development. Nash constructed the grand boulevard of Regent Street to connect the prince's home at **CARLTON HOUSE** to a new palace he intended to build in the centre of the park.

The sweeping terraces of grand houses were intended to be used by the prince's court and fashionable society. Unfortunately money ran out before the palace was begun.

In 1820 when he was king, George opened the Regent's Canal to further enhance the area's commercial value.

12 | **PRIMROSE HILL** North of Regent's Park NW3
Tel. (0171) 486 7905
Public access at all times
Free

The Prince Regent swapped royal land at Windsor with **ETON COLLEGE** for Primrose Hill. He wanted it for the grounds of his intended palace in Regent's Park.

Though the land was originally forest, it was cleared by **Elizabeth I** for shipbuilding at the time of the Spanish Armada.

13 | **16 CUMBERLAND TERRACE** NW1
Private

In keeping with her new role as the mistress of the Prince of Wales, Wallis Simpson moved here with financial help from the Prince.

14 | **33 CHESTER TERRACE** NW1
Private

When **Diana**'s parents separated, her mother moved in with her future husband, Shand-Kydd. The young Diana would often visit her mother here.

15 | **HALE CLINIC** 7 Park Crescent W1
Private

Diana comes once a month to this private clinic for a chiropractic massage with the medical director, Graham Heale. She has suffered from back pain since Prince Harry's birth.

16 | HARLEY STREET W1
Private
146 Harley Street
Lionel Logue had consulting rooms here in the 1930s when he helped **George VI** to overcome his terrible stammer.
149 Harley Street
Consulting rooms of Dr Anthony Dawson, the physician to the Queen.

17 | AINSWORTH'S 36 New Cavendish Street W1
This pharmacy supplies homeopathic medicines to the royal family.
　Prince Charles is a particular supporter of alternative medicine.

18 | 19 CLEVELAND STREET W1
Private
In the 1891, a homosexual brothel stood here.
　Queen Victoria's eldest grandson, Prince Albert Victor, was caught at the brothel along with the equerry of his brother (the future **George V**). Although homosexuality was illegal, the Prince was not charged. He died from typhoid at Sandringham in January 1892.

19 | ARDENT PRODUCTIONS Ariel House, Charlotte Street W1
Private
The offices of **Prince Edward**'s television production company.
　The company is backed financially by, amongst others, the Sultan of Brunei. Most of its work are documentaries on royal subjects. Edward can be seen here almost daily when not attending to his royal duties.

The City of London

This is the most ancient part of London. It has been in continual use since the Romans made it the centre of their administration. Parts of their wall marking out the city can be seen.

After the Romans' departure, English monarchs maintained the City's mercantile and military importance.

THE PRINCE AND PRINCESS OF WALES LEAVING ST PAUL'S CATHEDRAL ON THEIR WEDDING DAY

1 | ST PAUL'S CATHEDRAL EC4

Tel. (0171) 248 2705

Open Main Cathedral: Mon-Sat 8.30am-4.15pm (Other areas: daily 10.00am-4.00pm)

Admission charge

An ancient site of worship.

It first became Christian when the Saxon king, **Seebert**, built St Paul's Church in 604.

The medieval church was destroyed in the Great Fire of London in 1666 and Christopher Wren was commissioned to build the present cathedral. The construction took thirty-five years with the huge cost financed by a tax on all coal burnt in London.

A statue of **Queen Anne** stands outside St Paul's, during whose reign the cathedral was completed.

Prince Charles chose St Paul's for his wedding to **Lady Diana Spencer** on 29th July 1981. Although previous royal weddings had taken place at **WESTMINSTER ABBEY,** Charles believed its greater distance from **BUCKINGHAM PALACE** would allow more people to stand along the route. Diana was the first *English* woman to marry an heir to the throne since the time of Henry VIII.

Nearby is *Paternoster Square*. The choice of design for its rebuilding began **Prince Charles**'s campaign to reform British architecture along traditional lines.

2 | THE TOWER OF LONDON Tower Hill EC3

Tel. (0171) 709 0765

Open Mon-Sat 9am-6pm & Sun 10am-6pm (Nov-Feb: closes at 5pm)

Admission charge

The Tower of London has been used by the monarchy for nearly a thousand years as palace, fortress, armoury and prison.

Building began in 1067 when **William I** ordered a castle to be built at the south-east corner of the Roman city walls. By 1078 the keep dominated the city and its entry from the river. For safety, the royal apartments were on the top floor.

The long-lasting power struggles between **John** and his barons culminated in 1215 when they seized the castle and forced the king to sign the Magna Carta at RUNNYMEDE, Berkshire. However, the barons continued to distrust John and offered the throne to the French dauphin. Louis arrived and held court at the Tower for a year before **Henry III** came to the throne in 1216.

Henry III whitewashed the walls of the keep and it became known as the White Tower. He added the *Wakefield Tower* to make the castle a more spacious residence. A collection of exotic animals was built up: leopards from the German Emperor; an elephant from King Louis of France; and polar bears from the King of Norway.

In 1261 Henry lost control of England and shut himself in the Tower. When his queen, Eleanor, tried to escape the city by river, she was pelted with rubbish from London Bridge until forced to turn back.

By 1265, the king had regained power. In revenge, he imprisoned the mayor and gave the revenue from the shops and businesses on London Bridge to Eleanor.

The Tower became the monarch's treasury, where valuables were stored. It became the true centre of the power and the wealth of the King. Protests against the monarch therefore focused on the Tower.

Richard II began the tradition of spending the night before the coronation at the Tower. **Charles II** was the last monarch to follow the tradition in 1661. Since then no monarch has stayed over night in the Tower.

In 1399 Richard's traumatic reign ended when he was forced to abdicate the Crown in the Council Room, so becoming the first English king imprisoned in the Tower.

His successor, **Henry IV**, wished to bring some peace to the country and devised the Order of the Bath to symbolise this. He spent the night before his coronation at the Tower with forty-six of his followers. They had a ceremonial bath in St John's Chapel before the king knighted each of them. They then spent the rest of the night in prayer in the chapel.

THE TOWER AS PRISON

Over the centuries, many have been imprisoned or executed at the Tower.

■ **David II of Scotland** was held in 1346 after his defeat at the Battle of Neville's Cross.

■ In 1356, **King John of France** was imprisoned during the war with France. He was held along with his son, various members of his aristocracy and 2,000 knights. It took three years for his ransom to be raised.

■ **Henry VI** was captured in 1464 during the Wars of the Roses and was taken through London to the Tower on horseback wearing a straw hat and with a placard around his neck proclaiming his defeat. He was kept prisoner in the Wakefield Tower for six years with only a bible, a sparrow and a dog.

Later he was released and for a brief time was king again. After the Battle of Tewkesbury he was again imprisoned and later murdered in the *Wakefield Tower* on 21st May 1471 on the orders of his rival, **Edward IV**.

Every year on the anniversary of his death, representatives from **ETON COLLEGE** and **KINGS COLLEGE, CAMBRIDGE**, both of which he founded, put lilies and white roses, symbolising his House of Lancaster, on the spot where he was killed.

■ **Edward IV** also killed his brother, the Duke of Clarence, for treason against the Crown. The duke was drowned in a barrel of his favourite wine, Malmsey, in 1478 in the *Bowyer Tower*.

■ The twelve-year-old **Edward V** was killed in the Garden Tower (known as the Bloody Tower) in 1483 after a reign of less than a year. He was murdered along with his brother, allegedly on the orders of their uncle and guardian, the future **Richard III**.

In 1674 children's bones were discovered near the White Tower and they were reburied at **WESTMINSTER ABBEY** in the belief that they were 'the Princes in the Tower'.

■ **Henry VII**'s wife, Elizabeth of York, died in childbirth in the White Tower. Two wives of **Henry VIII** were executed for adultery: Anne Boleyn, who was buried in an arrow chest beneath the Chapel of St Peter ad Vincula, and Catherine Howard, who asked for the block on which she rehearsed her death the night before.

On her arrival at the Tower, she had seen the head of her lover, Thomas Culpepper, spiked on London Bridge. Her last words before dying were: "I die a queen, but I would rather die the wife of Culpepper."

Henry also ordered the executions of his chancellor Thomas Moore and archbishops Thomas Fisher and Thomas Cromwell.

■ **Mary I** imprisoned **Lady Jane Grey** who had claimed the throne for nine days.

Mary also imprisoned her sister (later **Elizabeth I**) for two months in the *Bell Tower* in 1554. She had been incriminated in a Protestant plot to overthrow the Catholic Mary after rebellions at the queen's unpopular announcement that she was to marry the Catholic King Philip of Spain.

Lady Jane Grey was executed but Elizabeth was released when the rebellions died down and no further evidence could be found against her.

Elizabeth returned to the Tower when she was proclaimed Queen in 1558.

■ **James I** imprisoned Sir Walter Raleigh in the *Bloody Tower* from 1603-1616 and Guy Fawkes was tortured in the Council Chamber before being hung, drawn and quartered for organising the Gunpowder Plot.

■ **Charles II**'s eldest illegitimate son, the Duke of Monmouth, was executed at the Tower in 1685 for an unsuccessful rebellion against his uncle, the Catholic **James II**.

The executioner's axe was blunt and the first blow failed causing the duke to stand up and rebuke the man. Again he tried and again he failed. In the end he was forced to complete the job with a knife.

■ Rudolph Hess, the deputy leader of Nazi Germany, was held here temporarily after being captured in May 1941. He was held in the *King's House*, where all distinguished prisoners were kept.

Queen Victoria opened the Tower to the public and by 1901, half a million visited it each year. The royal menagerie remained until 1834 when it moved to Regent's Park Zoo.

THE CEREMONY OF THE KEYS
daily 9.35-10.05pm (except Christmas Day)
Tickets can be applied for in writing, two months in advance, from:
Resident Governor, Queen's House, HM Tower of London EC3N 4AB
Free
Each night, the sentry and the Chief Yeoman Warder hand over the keys to lock up the Tower. The ceremony has taken place every day for over seven hundred years.

The Yeomen of the Guard were established in 1485 for the coronation of **Henry VII**. They are the oldest military corps in the world.

They are different from the Yeomen Warders of the Tower, who are known as the Beefeaters, and who were appointed by **Edward VI**.

3 | PEAT MARWICK MCLINTOCK Salisbury Square EC4
Private
Accountants to the royal family. Senior partner, Michael Peat audits the royal books.

4 | CASTLE BAYNARD STREET EC4
Site of a royal castle, which burnt down during the Great Fire of London in 1666.

Castle Baynard was built by **Henry I** in the twelfth century. **Edward IV** was proclaimed King here in 1461 and the castle was rebuilt by **Henry VII** in 1487.

Henry VIII maintained Castle Baynard for entertaining and as accommodation for his many wives. Anne of Cleves used the castle as her permanent London home.

In 1553 both **Lady Jane Grey** and then **Mary I** were proclaimed Queen at the castle.

5 | CORNEY & BARROW 12 Helmet Row EC1
Suppliers of wine to the Queen.

6 | SMITHFIELD MARKET EC1
From 1554-58 **Mary I** ordered the burning of over two hundred Protestants at the stake on the south-east corner of the square.

From these executions, she gained the nickname, 'Bloody Mary'. As a Catholic, Mary wanted to convert England back from Protestantism.

7 | THE GUILDHALL Guildhall Yard, off Gresham Street EC2

Tel. (0171) 606 3030

Open daily 9am-5pm

Free

In this fifteenth century city hall, **Victoria** made her first public appearance as queen when she attended the Lord Mayor's Banquet on 9th November 1837.

At the same occasion in 1992, **Elizabeth II** admitted for the first time the personal effects of the public outcry at her family's behaviour during her 'Annus Horribilis' speech.

8 | CROSBY SQUARE off Bishopsgate EC3

Richard III was proclaimed King in Crosby Hall in 1482. The hall, built by John Crosby, a wealthy city merchant, was moved to Cheyne Walk, SW10 in 1908.

THE COLLEGE
OF ARMS

9 | COLLEGE OF ARMS Queen Victoria Street EC4

Tel. (0171) 248 2762 for guided tours

Open Mon-Fri 10am-4pm

Free

The college records the lineage of the country's nobility. Though the monarch is known as 'the fountain of all honour', it is here that their coats of arms are created.

The Duke of Norfolk is the traditional Earl Marshall and he organises state occasions from here.

The building has been the home of Royal Heralds since the seventeenth century.

10 | PRINCE HENRY'S ROOM 17 Fleet Street EC4
Tel. (0171) 353 7323
Open Mon-Sat 11am-4pm
Free
Prince Henry was the eldest son of **James I**. He died in 1612 as Prince of Wales and his younger brother, Charles, inherited the throne.

In 1610, Henry stayed in the projecting upper storey above the gateway.

11 | UNILEVER HOUSE Victoria Embankment EC4
In 1515, **Henry VIII** built Bridewell Palace on this site, naming it after the nearby water-well of St Bride.

The king gave the palace to his illegitimate son, Henry Blount. The divorce negotiations between the king and Catherine of Aragon took place here in 1528 when Catherine saw the king for the last time.

Edward VI gave the palace to the City of London and it was destroyed by the Great Fire of London in 1666.

12 | CHRIST CHURCH GREYFRIARS (destroyed)
Newgate Street EC1
Destroyed in 1940, this Franciscan church was the burial place for several queens:
■ Eleanor of Provence, wife of **Henry III**, died in 1291 and her heart is buried here.
■ Margaret, wife of **Edward I**, in 1318
■ Isabella, wife of **Edward II**, in 1358, though her heart was taken to Gloucester Cathedral and placed in the tomb of her husband.

In 1538, **Henry VIII** dissolved the church and used it to store wine plundered from French ships.

13 | BUNHILL FIELDS EC1
In 1751, Frederick, Prince of Wales (father of **George III**) played cricket in these former fields. He was hit on the head by a ball and died a few days later.

Deer in royal **Richmond Park**

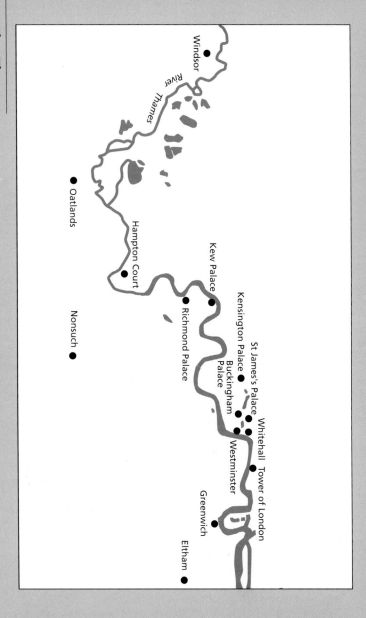

Windsor

River Thames

Oatlands

Hampton Court

Kew Palace

Nonsuch

Richmond Palace

Kensington Palace

St James's Palace

Buckingham Palace

Whitehall

Westminster

Tower of London

Greenwich

Eltham

South-east London

This area has long been a favourite of the royal family because of its closeness to both London and the east coast. Greenwich and Eltham were favoured homes due to their clean air and good hunting.

Like all the palaces in the Thames Valley, they were built on or near the river for fast and easy transport.

Greenwich (Saxon for 'green port') became important when the Romans built a road from London to Dover through the area.

It adjoins Blackheath (named both for its dark soil and as the burial place of plague victims) which was the site where monarchs were greeted on entering London: **Henry V** after his victory at Agincourt in 1415 and **Charles II** on his return to the throne in 1660.

1 | GREENWICH PALACE (demolished)
On site of Royal Naval College, King William Walk SE10

Henry V bought this section of land from the river up to Blackheath. On his death, his brother, the Duke of Gloucester, became Regent and built Bella Court on the land in 1433. Here he built up a library which he bequeathed to Oxford University. It forms the basis of the Bodleian Library.

He lent the house to his nephew, **Henry VI**, for his honeymoon with Margaret of Anjou. This generosity did not help him when in 1447, the duke was arrested by Henry, charged with treason and died in prison a few days later.

Henry VII rebuilt the palace and named it Placentia, 'the pleasant place'.

In 1491, **Henry VIII** was born here. On becoming king, he changed the name to Greenwich Palace. He added an armoury and a tilt-yard, to satisfy his passion for jousting.

Both Henry's daughters, Mary and Elizabeth, were born at Greenwich and baptised at the local church.

Elizabeth's mother, Anne Boleyn, first aroused the king's jealousy at a jousting tournament here when he saw her signalling to her lover. The following day she was arrested and taken to the TOWER OF LONDON. Henry signed her death warrant at Greenwich in May 1536.

Edward VI, Henry's heir, always physically weak, died of tuberculosis at the palace in 1553 aged sixteen.

Elizabeth I used Greenwich as a summer residence. She became known as the 'Virgin Queen' for her refusal to marry, although she enjoyed the attentions of several suitors.

It was here that her courtier, the explorer and poet Sir Walter Raleigh, famously laid his cloak over a puddle to protect her feet. He later impressed the court with his exotic exhibits from the Americas: tobacco and potatoes.

When at Greenwich, Elizabeth rode most days. However, this did not prevent her attending to affairs of state: in 1587 she signed the death warrant for **Mary, Queen of Scots** after returning from a hunt.

After Elizabeth's death, the palace was considered old and unfashionable and fell into disuse. During the Civil War, it was even turned it into a biscuit factory.

Charles II began to rebuild the palace in the 1660s. But with other demands on his limited finance, only one wing was completed.

In the 1690s, **William and Mary** had the building demolished and engaged Christopher Wren to use the stones for the construction of a hospital. This was given to the Navy in thanks for protecting the throne against the French.

The hospital became a Royal Naval College in 1873. **George V**, in his youth, spent one term at the college in 1884.

2 | **QUEEN'S HOUSE** Romney Road SE10
Tel. (0181) 858 5189
Open daily 10.00am-5.00pm (Oct-April: 10.30am-3.30pm)
Admission charge

After **James I** gave Greenwich Palace to his queen, Anne of Denmark, she instructed Inigo Jones, architect of the **BANQUETING HOUSE**, to build her a pleasure house. His H-shaped design linked the hunting park to the palace gardens and unusually stood over the public road to Woolwich.

The house was called the Queen's House after the tradition of it being given to the wife of the monarch.

In 1660 **Charles II** gave it to his queen, Catherine of Braganza. And when she failed to show interest, installed Jane Middleton, one of his mistresses.

In September 1714, the day before his coronation, the Hanoverian **George I** held his first reception in Britain here.

After the 1720s, the house fell into neglect and disrepute. Indeed one caretaker was executed for using the house as a centre for smuggling.

In 1805, the Queen's House was sold to the Royal Naval Hospital and has now been restored, forming part of the National Maritime Museum.

THE QUEEN'S HOUSE

GREENWICH PARK VIEW DOWN TO THE QUEEN'S HOUSE AND ACROSS THE RIVER

3 | GREENWICH PARK Charlton Way SE10

Tel. (0181) 858 2608
Open daily 5am-dusk
Free

Originally the park was part of the ancient forest of Anderida which stretched over much of south-east England.

In 1433 the Regent, Humphrey, Duke of Gloucester, enclosed two hundred acres to form a hunting park. The duke built a watchtower in the naturally fortified position on top of the hill.

The park ceased to be used for hunting when **James I** walled in the land in 1619. **Charles II** improved the park by planting over a thousand trees.

4 | ROYAL OBSERVATORY

Romney Road SE10
Tel. (0181) 858 4422
Open daily 10am-5pm
Admission charge

In 1675 **Charles II** demolished the watchtower and commissioned Christopher Wren to build the Royal Observatory.

Charles was a great sponsor of science (though less forthcoming with finance) and the observatory provided a place of research for, amongst other things, improved navigation, much needed by Britain's expanding naval power.

The zero meridian line, which divides the world into the eastern and western hemispheres, runs through the building. Greenwich Mean Time, established in 1880, originated at the observatory.

THE ROYAL OBSERVATORY AT THE TOP OF GREENWICH PARK: BRAINCHILD OF CHARLES II

5 | ELTHAM PALACE Court Yard, off Court Road, Eltham SE9
Tel. for opening times (0181) 294 2548
Admission charge

Eltham was a royal residence for three hundred years, though today only the Great Hall, with its giant hammer-beamed roof, remains.

The palace was built in 1295 by the Bishop of Durham, Anthony Bek, as his London retreat. The site was particularly desirable because it stood on elevated land with good air and fine views towards London, whilst remaining sheltered from cold north-easterly winds.

In 1305 Bek entertained the unstable Prince of Wales (later **Edward II**) at his retreat. The prince was so attracted to Eltham that he made it known that it would be in Bek's interest to make him a gift of the palace.

Edward's queen, Isabella, spent much time at Eltham, to be away from her husband, whom she hated and later had killed. Isabella brought up their son (later **Edward III**) at Eltham and he lived here as king, frequently holding parliaments in the palace buildings.

In 1347, during a jousting tournament, Edward's new Order of the Garter was made public for the first time.

Geoffrey Chaucer, author of the 'Canterbury Tales', was the Royal Clerk of Works during the reign of **Richard II** and frequently visited Eltham. During one visit, he was attacked and robbed.

Henry IV married Joan of Navarre in the palace in 1402.

In 1445, **Henry VI** hurriedly built the Great Hall for his new wife, Margaret of Anjou. However she seldom used Eltham, preferring to be closer to London at Greenwich.

During Christmas 1482, the unpopular **Richard III** (the last English king to die in battle) extravagantly entertained over two thousand noblemen in an attempt to win their favour.

Henry VIII was the last monarch to live at Eltham. Although born at Greenwich, he was brought up here. During the plague of 1526, he fled his court and London to spend Christmas at the palace in isolation.

Like her father, **Elizabeth I** was also born in Greenwich and brought up in Eltham. However during her youth, the moat became stagnant and the resulting sewerage made the palace unhealthy. She was moved to Hatfield and Eltham was abandoned.

During the Commonwealth, the park and trees were destroyed and the ruins dismantled for local buildings. The Great Hall survived as a barn until restored in the 1930s.

ELTHAM PALACE
THE HAMMER-BEAMED
ROOF OF THE
GREAT HALL

South-west London

1 | ELM HOUSE Parsons Green SW6
Private

Home of actress Dorothea Jordan, the mistress of **William IV**. She lived here with their ten children.

Despite this, the king died without legitimate issue and the throne passed to his niece, Victoria.

Maria Fitzherbert, the secret wife of **George IV**, lived opposite, in an Elizabethan house on the site of the flats at 17-41 Parsons Green.

2 | HARBOUR CLUB Water Meadow Lane SW6

This is **Diana**'s London gym.

In the early days of her marriage, Diana would swim daily at **BUCKINGHAM PALACE**. Today, she works out here up to four times a week.

Before the Harbour Club, Diana went to the LA Fitness Centre in West London, using the name Sally Hastings. But after secret photographs of her exercising appeared in the newspapers, she left.

The princess is 5'10" tall and weighs about 125 pounds. She wears size seven shoes and a size ten or twelve dress, depending on the designer. Her measurements are 35"/28"/35".

Also:

Vanderbilt Racquet Club, 31 Sterne Street W12

The princess plays tennis two or three times a week here.

Often she can be seen with her coach, Rex Seymour-Lyn.

CHISWICK HOUSE

3 | CHISWICK HOUSE Burlington Lane W4

Tel. (0181) 995 0508

Open daily 10am-6pm (Oct-March: Wed-Sun 10am-4pm)

Admission charge

Charles II gave the original Chiswick House to his eldest illegitimate son, the Duke of Monmouth.

But Monmouth soon sold the house for £4,000 and a captaincy in the socially prestigious Lifeguards regiment.

After Charles's death, the duke led an uprising against his Catholic uncle, **James II**. But his army was defeated at the battle of Sedgemoor and Monmouth was executed at the **TOWER OF LONDON** in 1685.

The present palladian villa was built in 1729 by William Kent for Lord Burlington.

In the mid-1860s, the Prince of Wales (later **Edward VII**) lived at Chiswick House before moving with his family to **MARLBOROUGH HOUSE** in St James's.

4 | WALPOLE HOUSE
Chiswick Mall W4
Private

The home of **Charles II**'s mistress, Barbara Villiers, after she had retired as the Duchess of Cleveland from royal service.

Villiers had born the king three sons, each of whom was given a dukedom. In addition, her husband had been compensated by the king with the title Earl of Castlemaine.

Barbara Villiers was buried at *St Nicholas's Church, Chiswick Mall* in 1709.

WALPOLE HOUSE

5 | RICHMOND PALACE (demolished)
On the site of Old Palace Lane, Richmond Green, Richmond
Private

Today, the gateway is all that survives of the palace.

Sheen (Anglo-Saxon for 'beautiful') has had royal associations since the twelfth century. The original palace, built in the fourteenth century, was home to several monarchs.

Edward III died at Sheen in 1377. It was said that at his death, his trusted mistress, Alice Perrers, turned against him. And as he lay dying, she organised the servants to strip his body of jewellery before calling in the priest to administer his last rites.

RICHMOND PALACE THE GATEWAY

The palace was destroyed by fire in 1498 and rebuilt by **Henry VII** in 1501. He called it Richmond after the earldom he had held before becoming king. His arms can be seen on the surviving gateway.

Henry came to the throne after decades of conflict had brought the country to near anarchy. During his reign, England enjoyed a long period of peace. He centralised the power of the monarchy and, through effective taxation, controlled the whole country.

At the time of his death here in 1509, the treasury vaults of Richmond held the then staggering sum of £1.8 million, making the Tudors one of the richest dynasties in Europe.

His heir, **Henry VIII**, used this money to turn the Court into one of the most lavish of its time.

Richmond Green was turned into a large jousting area and the palace hosted visits from several foreign monarchs, including Charles V, Emperor of Germany.

Ironically, it was during the Emperor's stay, that Henry noticed, for the first time, the even greater opulence of his chancellor, Wolsey, at **HAMPTON COURT**. The overspill of Charles V's large retinue was housed there and reports came back of the magnificence of the building. Against Richmond's two quadrangles, Hampton had five.

The king made the position clear: Wolsey duly made a 'gracious gift' and Henry moved to Hampton.

In 1540 Henry gave Richmond Palace to Anne of Cleves as part of her divorce settlement. But Henry remained a frequent visitor as, for a while, he considered the possibility of their remarriage.

Elizabeth I used Richmond for rest and recuperation. In her youth, the surrounding forest provided good hunting for the queen and her many suitors.

In her later years, she called the palace a "warm white box for my old bones" and it was a sanctuary from London. Elizabeth became increasingly superstitious and would frequently visit her alchemist and astrologer, Dr Dee, in the nearby village of *Mortlake*.

She feared aging and it is said that she never looked in a mirror between the ages of fifty and seventy. And when she did, whilst dressing at Richmond, the withered features so shocked her that she refused food, drink and even sleep.

Elizabeth became ill and retired to a bed in the room over the entrance gateway. As she grew delirious, she cried out for the return of her ex-lover, the Duke of Essex, beheaded on her orders two years before.

By the 23rd March 1603 she was suffering from a throat abscess and was unable to do more than nod her approval of **James VI** of Scotland as her successor. When she died later that night, her signet ring was dropped from the window to the waiting messenger below to take to Scotland with the news.

After the death of Elizabeth, subsequent monarchs kept the palace for family members and by the eighteenth century it had fallen to ruin.

Between them, the four Tudor monarchs had owned over eighty residences, but Richmond was always their favourite.

6 | OLD DEER PARK Richmond

The deer park was part of the grounds of **RICHMOND PALACE**.

A monastery for forty Carthusian monks was set up in the park and funded by **Henry V**. In exchange, the monks prayed for the atonement of his father, **Henry IV,** who had killed **Richard II**.

The monastery was dissolved in 1540.

MARBLE HILL HOUSE HOME OF ROYAL MISTRESSES

7 | MARBLE HILL HOUSE Richmond Road, Twickenham

Tel. (0181) 892 5115

Open daily 10am-6pm (Oct-March: Wed-Sun 10am-4pm)

Admission charge

George II built this palladian villa in 1723 for his mistress, Henrietta Howard, Countess of Suffolk. After the king's death, she helped Horace Walpole write 'Memoirs of the Reigns of George I and George II'.

Towards the end of the century, the Prince Regent (later **George IV**) placed his secret wife, Mrs Fitzherbert, in the house when he lived across the river at Kew.

8 | RICHMOND PARK

Tel. (0181) 948 3209

Open daily 5am-dusk

Free

Richmond Park was originally called New Park to distinguish it from Home Park next to **RICHMOND PALACE**. There are 2,740 acres of ancient forest land and it is about two miles wide.

Henry VIII frequently hunted here and *The Mound* at Petersham Gate was made for him to stand on during game drives. In 1536 the king stood on the mound to await the signal from London that Anne Boleyn, his second wife, had been executed. Views from the mound span ST PAUL'S CATHEDRAL to WINDSOR CASTLE.

Charles I enclosed the park in 1637 to enlarge the estate of RICHMOND PALACE. Though some was common land belonging to the citizens of East Sheen, none objected.

During the Commonwealth, the park was given to the City of London in return for their support during the Civil War.

Upon his restoration, **Charles II** retrieved the land and once again Richmond was used for hunting.

In the eighteenth century, the park fell into neglect. Only when **George II's** daughter, Princess Amelia, was made Ranger in 1751, did some royal interest return.

Today, deer still live in the park. Each autumn, several haunches of venison are traditionally distributed by the Crown to members of the Cabinet and to the Archbishops of Canterbury and York.

Richmond Park is home to several members of the royal family:
Thatched House Lodge Richmond Park
Private
This was the Ranger's house, built in 1673 and now the home of Princess Alexandra, a cousin of the Queen.

WHITE LODGE

White Lodge Richmond Park
Private
The house was built by **George I** and lived in by the wife of **George II**, Queen Caroline. She used to walk daily from the house to Richmond Hill, along what became known as *Queen's Ride*.

The Prince of Wales (later **Edward VII**) was sent to the lodge in 1857 to be educated privately, away from the temptations of the outer world. He was sixteen and spent a miserable time here with only two tutors and his equerries for company.

As a grieving widow, **Queen Victoria** came to live at the lodge for a short while in 1861.

PEMBROKE LODGE

Victoria's relations, the Teck family, then lived at the lodge for many years. The *Teck Plantation* in the centre of the park is named after them.

Princess May of Teck lived here before her marriage to the Duke of York (later **George V)**. She returned to give birth to her eldest son (the future **Edward VIII**) on 23rd June 1894.

When the next Duke of York (later **George VI**) married Elizabeth Bowes-Lyon, the White Lodge became their first home.

However, they considered it was too distant from London and soon moved to **145 PICCADILLY, W1**.

Pembroke Lodge Richmond Park
Pembroke Lodge, now the park's tea rooms, has the most spectacular views over the Thames.

George III gave the house in 1780 to his friend, the Countess of Pembroke. She lived here for fifty years. Then the Countess of Errol, lived here. She was the daughter of **William IV** and Mrs Jordan.

Queen Victoria gave the house to her Prime Minister, Lord John Russell. He disliked London so much that he frequently held Cabinet meetings here.

SYON HOUSE

9 | **SYON HOUSE** Syon Park, Park Road, Isleworth TW7
Tel. (0181) 560 0881
Open Wed-Sun 11.00am-4.15pm (Oct-March: Wed, Sat & Sun)
Admission charge
The site was originally a Bridgettine Monastery established by **Henry V** in 1415.
  Henry VIII dissolved the monastery and in 1541 imprisoned Catherine Howard, his fifth wife, here before her execution.

DOGS TEAR UP KING'S BODY
Although athletic in his youth, Henry degenerated physically during his last years until disease and excess made him too obese to walk.
  When he died in 1547 his bloated and poisoned body was taken from St James's to Windsor for burial. Unfortunately whilst resting overnight at Syon the body was left unattended. Dogs from the nunnery were attracted by what they considered easy pickings and tore into his carcass. When the king's stomach was pierced, gases were released that caused the royal body to partially explode.

The Duke of Northumberland became the Lord Protector to Henry's young son, **Edward VI**. Edward was weak and soon died. After his death, the duke attempted to place his daughter-in-law Lady Jane Grey on the throne rather than Edward's sister, the Catholic **Mary I**. However, within nine days the coup had failed and Northumberland, his son and daughter-in-law were sent to the **TOWER OF LONDON** for execution.
  Elizabeth I gave Syon House in 1594 to the Percy family, the Dukes of Northumberland, back in favour with the Crown. The present house was built in 1761 by Robert Adams and with gardens by Capability Brown.

10 | KEW PALACE Royal Botanic Gardens, Kew

Tel. (0181) 940 1171

Open April-Sept: daily 11.30am-5.30pm

Admission charge

Built in 1631, the palace was originally known as the Dutch House, because of its gabled roof.

In the early 1720s, the Prince of Wales (later **George II**) made Kew fashionable when he bought Richmond Lodge in the adjoining **OLD DEER PARK**.

In 1727 he ascended the throne and a year later, his wife, Caroline, leased the Dutch House to develop a garden.

Their son, Frederick, the Prince of Wales, lived in the neighbouring, and now demolished, White House. Though he disliked his parents intensely, he remained there until his death in 1751.

Frederick's son, as **George III**, returned to the White House with his family of fifteen children. Because of the small size of the house, they also used the Dutch House, particularly as the king was passionate about gardening.

George's wife, Charlotte, brought many traditions to England from her native Germany. Amongst these was the 'Christmas Tree', which she first installed in the Dutch House.

KEW PALACE

ROYAL MARRIAGES

In 1817 an altar was placed in the first floor drawing room so that the royal Dukes of Clarence, Cambridge and Kent could each marry in haste.

The reason was that their father **George III** was close to death and their brother the Prince Regent (later **George IV**) was childless. And so it was up to one of them to produce if England was to have a clear heir. Besides, parliament had offered a large stipend and the paying off of all debts to whoever could produce first.

The Duke of Kent was the only brother to achieve success with Princess Victoire of Saxe-Coburg-Saalfeld, a widow with two children. Nine months after their marriage, a daughter was born: Victoria. The duke died eight months later.

11 | KEW ROYAL BOTANIC GARDENS

Tel. (0181) 332 5000
Open daily 9.30am-dusk
Admission charge

Caroline, wife of **George II**, first developed the garden when she moved to the Dutch House.

All purchases were made from her own purse. The extravagant use of follies and exotic plants led her into debts of £20,000. However, they form the foundations of today's gardens.

George III built the *Queen's Cottage* as a summerhouse for both shooting and picnics.

Unfortunately he suffered from periods of madness. During one of these periods, he was confined at Kew, where he worked in the gardens. His ministers would visit him frequently to monitor his recovery. Once they arrived to be informed by the king that the country's meat shortage had been solved through his cultivation of a 'beef plant' and he showed them a 'crop' of snails.

Queen Victoria gave the gardens to the public in 1841. However, she retained the Queen's Cottage until 1897 as she enjoyed holding tea-parties in the elaborate two-storied, thatched summerhouse.

HAMPTON COURT PALACE THE TUDOR GATEWAY

12 | HAMPTON COURT PALACE East Molesey, Surrey

Tel. (0181) 781 9500

Open daily 9.30am-6.00pm (Oct-March: closes at 4.30pm)

Admission charge

Cardinal Wolsey gave **Henry VIII** Hampton Court Palace in 1526 to try to prevent his fall from power. During the previous 14 years, Wolsey had built it into a luxurious palace of 280 rooms requiring over 500 servants. He had been the most powerful man in the country after the king.

   Henry VIII added to the building and redecorated it as a fitting symbol of his powerful reign. The kings's apartments were on the first floor. Above him were the rooms of his wife, Catherine of Aragon; and their daughter (later **Mary I**) lived on the ground floor.

   After his marriage to Anne Boleyn, Henry gave his new wife a manor house at Hanworth (on the site of *Hanworth Park House*) instead of apartments at Hampton Court.

   Before his physical decline in middle age, Henry was very active and particularly fond of sports. To these ends he built a real tennis court and three bowling alleys for his own use. He also built a tilt yard for jousting practice and tournaments.

   His third wife, Jane Seymour, died at Hampton Court on 14th October 1537 shortly after giving birth to his only male heir (later **Edward VI**).

Mary I used Hampton Court for her honeymoon with King Philip of Spain. However, the time was brief for within days he had left to return to Spain.

   Seventy-five years later, **Charles I** brought his fifteen year old French bride, Henrietta Maria, to the palace for their honeymoon. And his son, **Charles II** came with Catherine of Braganza for theirs thirty-seven years later.

During the later part of the Civil War in 1647, **Charles I** fled Hampton Court by the river to escape capture, just ahead of his approaching enemies. But within days, he was caught and held at CARISBROOKE CASTLE on the Isle of Wight and the Civil War was effectively over.

In 1689, **William and Mary** were crowned Britain's only joint monarchs. They were offered the throne as a solution to the Catholic-Protestant conflict at the end of **James II**'s reign. However, their power was limited by the 1688 Bill of Rights, making them the forerunners of the modern constitutional monarchy.

   William came from the Netherlands and with his Dutch court introduced gin and the tulip.

   They wanted to use Hampton Court but it had fallen into disuse and the dark and small rooms of the Tudor palace had become unfashionable. The leading London architect, Christopher Wren, was engaged to restore the building to its former magnificence. To do this, Wren planned to demolish and replace the old palace.

   However when Mary died in 1689, William stopped the work, with only the Tudor state apartments demolished and two new wings completed: the Park Block and the Privy Gate Block.

During the eighteenth century, the Hanoverian monarchs used Hampton Court as a family residence. Particularly **George I**, who did not speak English and preferred to retreat to Hampton Court rather than feeling ill at ease amongst his foreign subjects in London.

His great-grandson **George III** visited Hampton only occasionally. The palace contained memories of humiliation for him as his grandfather, **George II**, had frequently beaten him in front of the court.

Gradually, the palace lost its royal residents and became accommodation for favoured servants and retainers. One of them, the landscape gardener, Capability Brown, planted the Great Vine in 1769.

William IV restored the state apartments and opened them to the public in the early 1830s.

Today the only regular royal to use Hampton Court is the Queen's youngest son, **Prince Edward**, who uses the Tudor tennis court for his Real Tennis Tournaments.

13 | BUSHY PARK opposite Hampton Court Palace
Open daily 5am-dusk
Free
In 1526 Cardinal Wolsey gave Bushy Park to **Henry VIII** along with **HAMPTON COURT**.

In the 1680s, Christopher Wren laid out the Chestnut Walk and built the Diana fountain as part of his redesign of the palace. But the thousand acre park remains essentially as it has always been, open land for deer.

Bushy House, on the outskirts of the park, was built by Lord Halifax in the eighteenth century and was occupied by the rangers of the park. The Duke of Clarence (later **William IV**) lived for a time at Bushy House.

14 | KINGSTON-UPON-THAMES
Kingston is named after the King's Stone, which stands in front of the Guildhall.

The stone was used for the coronations of at least seven Saxon kings of southern England. The last king to be crowned here was **Ethelred the Unready** in 979AD.

North London

1 | **LAUDERDALE HOUSE** Waterlow Park, Highgate N6
Tel. (0181) 348 8716
Open Tue-Fri 11am-4pm & Sun 12-5pm
Free
Charles II leased Lauderdale House as a summer residence for his mistress, Nell
Gwynne.

> THE MAKING OF A HEREDITARY PEER
> Whilst Charles was visiting her at Lauderdale House, Nell called their son to
> her: "Come here you little bastard". When the king complained at her
> language, she said, "He is a bastard. What else can I call him?" She then held
> the boy outside the window and threatened to drop him because the king
> showed no interest in his offspring. Alarmed, Charles shouted "God save the
> Earl of Burford!"
>   The earl was later made the Duke of St Albans and until 1956, his heirs
> continued to sit in the House of Lords

2 | **ENFIELD PALACE (ruins)**
On site of Church Street, Enfield EN1
The remains of **Henry VIII**'s palace are opposite the church on the
present day Church Street.
   Enfield Palace passed to Henry from Sir Thomas Lovell, speaker of the
House of Commons. The palace was used frequently after **ELTHAM PALACE**
in south-east London had become unhealthy. Henry's children, Mary, Elizabeth
and Edward, were all raised here.
   Edward VI was proclaimed king in the palace garden. His first decision
was to choose the Duke of Somerset as his Lord Protectorate until he became
of age. Somerset was soon ousted by the Duke of Northumberland.
   His sister, **Elizabeth I**, used the palace for hunting and relaxing.
But after her reign, Enfield fell into disuse.

HEVER CASTLE

Castle
of Mey

SCOTLAND

Balmoral

Glamis
Castle

Stirling
Castle

Edinburgh
Castle

Palace of
Holyroodhouse

ENGLAND

Caernarfon

Sandringham

Audley
End

WALES

Hatfield
House

Highgrove

Guildford
Castle

Winchester

Brighton
Pavilion

Osborne
House

Kent

1 | CHEVENING
Private

In April 1974, **Prince Charles** was given Chevening as his first country house. He felt it was too large for his needs and did not use it.

It is now the country residence of the Foreign Secretary.

KNOLE HOUSE

2 | SEVENOAKS
Knole House
Tel. (01732) 450608
Open April-Oct: Wed-Sun 11am-5pm (Thurs 2-5pm)
Admission charge

Henry VIII was given Knole by the Archbishop of Canterbury, Thomas Cranmer, in 1538. But the king only visited it once.

In 1561, his daughter, **Elizabeth I**, gave the house to Dudley, the Earl of Leicester, her favourite nobleman. However, within a few years, Dudley had fallen from grace and was executed. Elizabeth then gave Knole to the Sackville family.

West Heath School, outside Sevenoaks
Diana, Princess of Wales, went to this school.

Though she became proficient in swimming and dancing, Diana failed to gain any exams.

Sevenoaks School
Princess Anne's second husband, Tim Lawrence, went to school here. After a degree at Durham University, he joined the Navy. Later he became an equerry to the Queen and met Princess Anne.

3 | LEEDS CASTLE Maidstone
Tel. (01622) 765400
Open daily 11.00am-5.30pm (Nov-Feb: 10.15am-3.30pm)
Admission charge

Leeds Castle was first built as a wooden fortress by a Saxon named Leed. After the Conquest, the Normans rebuilt the castle in stone.

LEEDS CASTLE

Edward I took possession of the castle on his accession and gave it to his queen, Eleanor. It remained a royal palace for the next three hundred years.

The widow of **Henry IV**, Joan of Navarre, spent the last part of a three-year sentence for witchcraft at the castle.

Henry V's widow, Catherine de Valois, stayed at the castle after his death. Whilst living here, she employed Owen Tudor as Clerk of the Wardrobe. They fell in love and, despite the scandal, married. Their son, Edmund, was the father of **Henry VII**, the first of the Tudor monarchs.

Henry VIII used Leeds on route to Dover and he built the banqueting hall and royal chapel.

4 | CHATHAM HISTORIC DOCK YARD Chatham

Tel. (01634) 812551
Open daily 10am-5pm (Nov-March: Wed & weekends 10am-4pm) Closed Dec
Admission charge

Henry VIII established the Royal Dockyards at Woolwich in 1512 and is known as the father of the British Navy, after he built the largest ship of its time, 'the Great Harry'.

Elizabeth I moved the Royal Docks to Chatham on her father's death.

5 | CANTERBURY CATHEDRAL Canterbury

Tel. (01227) 762862
Open daily 9am-5pm (summer: closes at 7pm)
Admission charge

St Augustine was sent from Rome to persuade the Saxon king **Ethelbert** to convert to Christianity. He succeeded and Kent became the first Christian kingdom in England with Canterbury established as the country's premier bishopric.

On 29th December 1170, **Henry II** ordered the murder of the Archbishop of Canterbury and his ex-chancellor, Thomas Becket, for opposing the king's plans to reduce Church power in England. The death of Becket caused such an outcry that Henry was forced to accept the penance of walking barefoot to the cathedral gates and there being publicly flogged by the priests.

Royal connections have remained with the cathedral:

- **Henry III** married Eleanor of Provence at the cathedral on 20th January 1236.
- **Henry IV**, his wife Joan of Navarre, and the Black Prince (son of **Edward III**) are buried here.
- **Charles I** married Henrietta Maria here on 13th June 1625.

6 | DOVER CASTLE Dover
Tel. (01304) 201628
Open daily 10am-4pm
Admission charge

Dover Castle was built by **Henry II** to guard this narrowest strip of the Channel from French invasion.

After Dover was besieged by the French during the reign of **King John**, his successor, **Henry III**, fortified the castle even further to a total of 17 towers. Most of the tops of these towers were dismantled during the Second World War to allow anti-air guns to be erected.

7 | HEVER CASTLE Hever, near Edenbridge
Tel. (01732) 865224
Open March-Nov: daily 12-6pm (grounds open at 11am)
Admission charge

Family home of Anne Boleyn, second wife of **Henry VIII**.

Anne had been a lady-in-waiting to Henry's first wife, Catherine of Aragon, when she caught the king's eye. Her elder sister had already been his mistress and Anne was at first reluctant to be seduced.

In 1533, Henry divorced Catherine and sent her to Kimbolton Castle in Cambridgeshire, where she died three years later and was buried at Peterborough Cathedral.

Once divorced, Henry married Anne and within a year she had given birth to a daughter (later **Elizabeth I**).

Her father, Sir Thomas, benefited greatly from the royal marriage. He changed the family name from Bullen to the grander Boleyn and started to accrue income from favours granted.

However within three years, it was over. Anne had fallen from favour. On 29th January 1536 she gave birth to a still-born son (coincidentally the same day as the funeral of Catherine of Aragon). She was accused by Henry of treason and of incest with her brother. In May, Anne was executed at the Tower of London, having been denounced by both her father and uncle, the Duke of Norfolk.

Two years later, Sir Thomas died and Henry took possession of Hever.

Henry sent Anne of Cleves, his fourth wife, to the castle after their divorce. She lived at Hever for seventeen years until her death in 1557.

The castle fell into ruin until it was rebuilt in the twentieth century.

8 | BENENDEN SCHOOL Benenden
Private

Princess Anne went to this leading girls school in the 1960s.

Surrey

1 | GUILDFORD CASTLE Guildford
Tel. (01483) 444751
Open Easter-Sept: daily 10am-5pm
Admission charge
The remains of Guildford Castle stand on the banks of the River Wey in the middle of the city. The castle dates from the Saxon kings who used it as an important fortified home.

The castle was captured in 1216 by King Louis of France, just as **Henry III** ascended the throne. Henry won back the fortress and made Guildford the capital of the area. The castle became his favourite residence because the surrounding land provided good hunting. He decreed that the area should remain as a hunting forest.

Edward I modernised the castle to better house his family. But by the late fifteenth century, at the time of the Tudor monarchs, Guildford was out-dated and the castle fell into ruin.

2 | POLESDEN LACEY Great Bookham
Tel. (01372) 458203
Open Wed-Sun 1.30-5.30pm (Nov-March: Sat only)
Admission charge
The Duke of York (later **George VI**) honeymooned with Elizabeth Bowes-Lyon (later **the Queen Mother)** at this regency villa in 1923.

3 | NONSUCH PALACE (demolished)
Nonsuch Park, London Road, Cheam
Only a few markings in the ground remain of the once magnificent Tudor hunting palace of Nonsuch.

Henry VIII wanted to rival the French king's chateau at Chambord. He called his 'Nonsuch' to imply that no palace could better it.

Set in two thousand acres of hunting park, the palace consisted of two richly decorated courts, with their stone from monasteries dissolved during the Reformation. The site of the palace was on the demolished village of Cuddlington. Despite its magnificence, the palace was quite small, being only about 150 yards in length.

Henry was the only monarch to spend time at Nonsuch:
- **Mary I** disliked the opulence and leased it to the Earl of Arundel.
- **Elizabeth I** took it back in 1591, but rarely used it.
- **The Stuarts** found it eerie, although exotic and **Charles II** gave it to his mistress, Barbara Villiers, who promptly pulled the dilapidated palace down and sold it off in separate lots.

Lady Castlemaine, Duchess of Cleveland

4 | OATLANDS HOUSE (demolished)

On the site of Oatlands Hotel, Oatlands Park, Oatlands Drive, Weybridge

Private

Henry VIII originally bought the land to incorporate into the estate of Hampton Court. On 28th July 1540, he married Catherine Howard at the manor house.

After his reign, Oatlands fell into disuse, except for a brief time when the wife of **James I** set up a silkworm factory in the garden.

5 | CLAREMONT PARK Portsmouth Road, Esher

Tel. (01372) 469421

Open daily 10am-sunset

Admission charge

Claremont House was built by Vanbrugh in 1772 for Clive of India, with gardens designed by Capability Brown.

In 1816, the house was bought for **George III**'s daughter, Charlotte, when she married Prince Leopold Battenberg of Saxe-Coburg-Saalfeld. Princess Charlotte's death in childbirth made **Victoria** the heir to the throne.

During her childhood and early marriage, Victoria frequently visited her uncle Leopold at the house, until he left to become King of Belgium.

As queen, Victoria bought the house in 1881 for her son, the Duke of Albany.

6 | CHEAM PREPARATORY SCHOOL Cheam

In 1957, **Prince Charles** came to the school for a short time. He was following the pattern set by his father, **Prince Philip**, who had also attended the school.

Charles was made the Captain of the football team, though they lost every match.

The school has now moved to Headly in Berkshire.

7 | EPSOM DOWNS RACECOURSE Ashley Road, Epsom Downs

Tel. (01372) 726311

Monarchs have patronised racing here since the eighteenth century. Epsom is the home of the Derby and the royal family continue the tradition by attending the meeting every June.

Sussex

1 | **BATTLE ABBEY** Battle, East Sussex
Tel. (01424) 773792
Open daily 10am-6pm (Nov-March: closes at 4pm)
Admission charge
William the Conqueror built the abbey to commemorate his victory over the Saxons.

The altar stands on the site where **Harold** was clubbed to death after the Norman invaders broke his shield-wall on 14th October 1066.

2 | **PEVENSEY CASTLE** Pevensey, East Sussex
Tel. (01323) 762604
Open daily 10am-6pm (Nov-March: closes at 4pm)
Admission charge
William the Conqueror landed at Pevensey on 28th September 1066. After his victory at Hastings, he ordered a castle to be built to defend his new kingdom.

The castle used to stand on the edge of the sea, but changes in the shoreline have left it landlocked.

3 | **ASHDOWN HOUSE SCHOOL** Forest Row, East Sussex
Private
Princess Margaret sent her eldest son, David Linley, here for a short period in the mid 1960s.

THE ROYAL PAVILION

4 | **THE ROYAL PAVILION** Brighton, West Sussex
Tel. (01273) 603005
Open daily 10am-6pm (Oct-May: closes at 5pm)
Admission charge
The Prince Regent (later **George IV**) first visited Brighton in 1783.
He needed a break from creditors in London and doctors had suggested the sea-air would benefit his health.

For several summers he leased a farmhouse on this site and much to his surprise, fell in love with the area.

In 1800 after a few years of relative economy, he bought the land and engaged John Nash to build the Pavilion. No expense was spared. The designs mixed Indian, Gothic and Chinese styles.

Fashionable Society moved to Brighton for the Season. Exotic balls and garden parties were held. But the prince never used the beach, let alone swam in the sea. Instead he had a room built with a deep bath, into which sea-water was pumped.

The expense of the Pavilion, along with that of **CARLTON HOUSE** in London, increased his debts to over half a million pounds. After ascending the throne in 1820, he hardly used the Pavilion again.

When **Queen Victoria** inherited the property, she promptly sold it to the town of Brighton to fund the building of **OSBORNE HOUSE** on the Isle of Wight.

5 | DITCHLING West Sussex
Anne of Cleves, fourth wife of **Henry VIII**, was given a home here as part of her divorce settlement from the king.

Prince Charles's mistress, Camilla Parker-Bowles, went to Dumbrells School in the village when her family lived at 'The Laines' in the nearby village of Plumpton.

Camilla's great-great-grandmother was Alice Keppel, who was the mistress of Prince Charles's great-great-grandfather, **Edward VII**.

6 | GOODWOOD RACECOURSE Midhurst, West Sussex
Tel. (01243) 779922
Racing May-Sept
Goodwood House open Easter-Sept: tel. (01243) 774107
Charles II's illegitimate son, the Duke of Richmond, bought Goodwood House as a hunting lodge in 1697.

The 'Glorious Goodwood' flat racing meeting is held every July and the Queen and members of the royal family always attend.

The Queen has often stayed at the house, still home to the Dukes of Richmond, and has even held Privy Councils here.

7 | COWDRAY PARK Midhurst, West Sussex
Tel. (01730) 812089
Prince Charles plays regularly with his team at Cowdray Polo Park during the season, May to September.

8 | CRAIGWELL HOUSE Aldwick, Bognor Regis, West Sussex
Private
George V convalesced from bronchial pneumonia at this house in 1929 just outside the seaside resort of Bognor. He was visited often by his favourite granddaughter, Princess Elizabeth.

The town added 'Regis' to its name to commemorate the royal association.

9 | ARUNDEL CASTLE Arundel, West Sussex

Tel. (01903) 882173

Open Easter-Oct: daily 12-5pm

Admission charge

This romantic Norman castle is the seat of the Dukes of Norfolk.

The Dukedom of Norfolk is the premier non-royal dukedom in England and it also holds the post of Earl Marshal of England.

The Earl Marshal is responsible for managing the great state occasions, including coronations, investitures and funerals.

The Queen used to stay at Arundel Castle during the Goodwood races.

10 | BOSHAM near Chichester, West Sussex

Here, according to legend, **King Canute** sat on the beach and ordered the incoming tide not to advance.

The enlightened Saxon king ruled at the beginning of the eleventh century. His gesture was to prove to his subjects that kings did not possess God-like powers.

Hampshire

1 | WINCHESTER CASTLE off High Street, Winchester

Tel. (01962) 841841

Open daily 10am-5pm (winter: closes 4pm)

Admission charge

In the ninth century **Alfred the Great** made Winchester the capital of his Saxon kingdom of Wessex. He is buried at the castle, as is **King Canute**. Winchester vied with London as the capital of England until losing out in the thirteenth century.

Henry III was born in Winchester Castle in 1207.

Only the Great Hall remains from its destruction during the Civil War in 1645.

Winchester was believed to be King Arthur's mythological court, Camelot. In 1265, **Edward I** had a one-tonne table built to reproduce the Round Table. It still hangs on the wall of the Great Hall.

2 | NEW FOREST

Public access at all times

William I, after conquering England, regarded Winchester as the capital, because of its proximity to the south coast.

Whilst at Winchester, he began the planting of a hunting forest, which became known as the New Forest.

His unpopular heir, **William Rufus**, was killed on 2nd August 1100 in the forest by an arrow, probably on the orders of his younger brother, who became **Henry I**.

3 | BROADLANDS Romsey

Tel. (01794) 516878

Open Easter-Oct: daily 10.00am-5.30pm (closed Fri)

Admission charge

Broadlands, just outside the New Forest, was the home of Victoria's Prime Minister, Lord Palmerston.

In the mid-twentieth century, it became home to Lord Mountbatten, uncle of Prince Philip. In 1947, Princess Elizabeth (later **Elizabeth II**) and Prince Philip spent the first nights of their honeymoon here.

Today it is the home of Lord Romsey, a close friend of **Prince Charles** and godfather to Prince William. Charles and Diana spent the first night of their honeymoon at Broadlands.

Isle of Wight

Queen Victoria bought a country retreat, or 'marine residence' as she called it, on this holiday island.

The **Duke of Edinburgh** and **Princess Anne** are amongst several members of the royal family who attend the sailing regatta during Cowes Week. The centre of royal activity at this time is the Royal Yacht Club on the harbour-front.

1 | **OSBORNE HOUSE** East Cowes
Tel. (01983) 200022
Open Easter-Oct: daily 10am-6pm
Admission charge

During the 1840s, **Queen Victoria** and **Prince Albert** began to dislike living in London. Life with their growing family was becoming particularly unpleasant in the very public, and unhealthy, **Buckingham Palace**. In addition, the queen had been the focus of political dissent and several assassination attempts.

In 1845 Victoria bought a thousand acres of woodland and a beach here. Albert engaged Thomas Cubitt, the builder of Belgravia, to rebuild the existing house. It was financed by the economies he had made at **Buckingham Palace** and the sale of **Brighton Pavilion**.

Both Albert and Victoria took personal interest in the planning and construction. They kept the house relatively small so as to create a family atmosphere and it was only in 1891 that the Durbar Room was added for grander entertaining.

The royal family spent each summer here. The children learnt about house management and gardening when Albert built the Swiss Cottage in the grounds. The royal children were taught to understand money through the growing and selling of vegetables.

Queen Victoria at
Osborne House

After Albert's death in 1861, Victoria spent longer periods of time at Osborne, to the irritation of her ministers who frequently had to make the long journey on state business.

When the queen died on 22nd January 1901, she lay in state in the dining room. The room was covered in white cloth as was her body, adorned with her wedding veil - a stark contrast to the black she had worn for the past forty years.

Albert's dressing gown was placed in her coffin, along with a plaster cast of his hand and family photographs, including one of John Brown, her Scottish manservant.

The coffin was taken to **BUCKINGHAM PALACE**, and then to Windsor to join Albert's tomb at **FROGMORE MAUSOLEUM**.

Edward VII inherited Osborne. He considered it morbid and gave it to the nation to use as a convalescence home leaving the state apartments open to the public.

Elizabeth II opened the private apartments for viewing. The house today is left as it was on Queen Victoria's death.

2 | **CARISBROOKE CASTLE** Newport

Tel. (01983) 522107
Open Easter-Oct: daily 10am-6pm
Admission charge

Carisbrooke Castle was built on the site of a Roman Fort.

Charles I was imprisoned here for 14 months in 1647 after temporarily escaping the Parliamentarian forces at **HAMPTON COURT**.

A planned rescue of Charles failed when he got stuck between the bars of a window.

It was from Carisbrooke that he journeyed back to London to face trial and execution.

In the nineteenth century **Queen Victoria**'s youngest daughter, Princess Beatrice, lived at the castle when she was made Governor of the Isle of Wight.

South-west England

1 | **JOHN MAKEPEACE SCHOOL** Parnham, Dorset
Private
David Linley, the son of **Princess Margaret**, studied carpentry here before starting his cabinet-making business in London.

2 | **CHIDEOCK MANOR** near Bridport, Dorset
Private
The first married home of the Duke and Duchess of York.
    Prince Andrew and Sarah rented the house for weekends whilst Sᴜɴɴɪɴɢʜɪʟʟ Pᴀʀᴋ in Berkshire was being built.

3 | **DARTMOUTH NAVAL COLLEGE** Dartmouth, Devon
Private
Edward VIII and **George VI** both attended Dartmouth College.
    Their father, **George V**, had been the youngest ever cadet when he came to the college at the age of twelve.
    In July 1939, Princess Elizabeth (later **Elizabeth II**) met Prince Philip for the first time, when he was the cadet chosen to escort her around the college.

Richard I left from Dartmouth to go to the Middle East on the crusades in the twelfth century.

4 | **WOOLBROOK COTTAGE** Woolbrook Glen, Sidmouth, Devon
Private
The Duke of Kent, father of **Queen Victoria**, died here in 1819, leaving his widow and daughter in debt.
    His financial troubles were the result of high living, gambling and his mistress of 27 years, Therese-Bernadine Margaret of Besancon.
    The duke had bought Therese-Bernadine, Castle Hill House in Ealing as well as an apartment in Knightsbridge. These properties eventually had to be sold to help pay off his debts.

5 | **SCILLY ISLES** off the coast of Cornwall
Prince Charles has a retreat on the islands where he chooses to live simply for peace and contemplation.
    As heir to the throne, Charles is also the Duke of Cornwall, an ancient title created to provide the Prince of Wales with an income.
    The estate owns extensive land in the West Country including Dartmoor and the Scilly Isles.

WINDSOR CASTLE

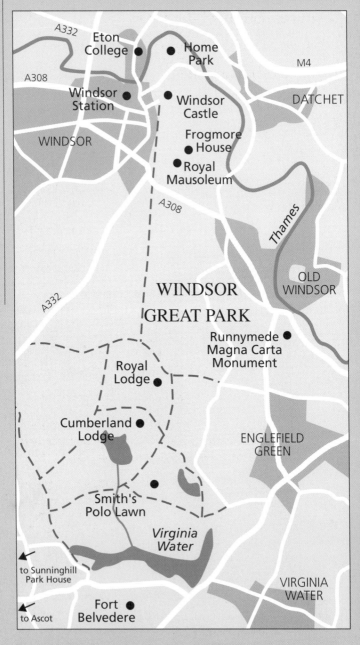

The Royal County of Berkshire

Berkshire's association with the monarchy goes back over a thousand years. Windsor has been one of the country's major fortifications since the eleventh century and many of **Elizabeth II**'s immediate family live in the surrounding area.

1 | WINDSOR CASTLE
Tel. (01753) 868286
Open daily 10am-5pm (winter: closes at 4pm)
Admission charge
Windsor Castle is the longest continuous Royal residence.

The name Windsor comes from the Saxon word 'Windlesora', meaning 'winding river bank'. Saxon kings first built a castle at Kingsbury, on the river in Old Windsor. This existed until 1110.

THE HISTORY
The present castle began as a fortified mound built by **William the Conqueror** in 1080. He used the Norman keep as a base for hunting in the area.

Henry I built a more permanent residence; **Henry II** added luxury and extended defences to include the moat and outer walls. **Henry III** strengthened the castle further by building the first Round Tower in 1272.

Edward III was the first monarch born at Windsor Castle. As king, he built the royal apartments in a quadrangle, a tradition that has continued.

Elizabeth I rebuilt the North Terrace. But, like all monarchs before the seventeenth century, she could only spend a short time in one place as poor communications required her to travel throughout the country.

During the Civil War, Windsor Castle became a military headquarters and prison.

Upon the restoration of the monarchy, **Charles II** used Windsor as a country residence. He rebuilt and redesigned the royal apartments, the Star Building and St George's Hall. In addition in 1685, he set out the Long Walk from the castle through Windsor Great Park.

After his reign, Windsor was used less frequently: **Anne** stayed at the Queen's Lodge in Home Park for her summer retreat, but seldom ventured into the castle.

The **Hanoverians** preferred HAMPTON COURT. However, **George III** was kept at Windsor Castle during the last years of his madness on the orders of his son, the Prince Regent. He died here in 1820 both deaf and blind.

Previously George had resided at the Queen's Lodge only using the castle for state occasions.

The Prince Regent (later **George IV**) rarely came to Windsor during his father's madness. This was partly due to having been attacked and hit over the head by the deranged king during a state banquet at the castle. If he had to visit, he stayed at the ROYAL LODGE in the Great Park.

When the Prince Regent became king, he demolished the Queen's Lodge and set about renovating the castle. The cost was astronomical. Banqueting rooms, Gothic apartments, the Waterloo chamber and the Round Tower were all modernised with many furnishings and fixtures coming from CARLTON HOUSE.

In 1830, **George IV** died at Windsor from liver damage caused by years of excess.

QUEEN VICTORIA

Victoria made Windsor Castle central to the life of the monarchy.

She proposed to Prince Albert here and when married, would regularly spend weekends at Windsor, setting the pattern for future sovereigns.

On 14th December 1861, Albert died in the Blue Drawing Room. After this, Victoria withdrew from public life. She spent more time here and became known as 'the Widow of Windsor'. The Albert Memorial Chapel was rebuilt in her husband's memory.

During these years, Victoria became close to her Scottish servant, John Brown, after he had saved her from assassination outside an entrance to **BUCKINGHAM PALACE**. Their friendship led to rumours of a relationship and the newspapers nicknamed her 'Mrs Brown'. After his death, she ordered a flower to be placed daily in his old room in the Clarence Tower. This was carried out until her own death in 1901.

THE TWENTIETH CENTURY

Edward VII did not use Windsor Castle. He associated the place with his mother's long period of mourning and much preferred the sporting attractions of **SANDRINGHAM**.

During the First World War, **George V** changed the family name to Windsor as a result of public resentment to their German name, Saxe-Coburg-Gotha. Windsor, with the monarch's long association, was considered the most appropriate.

Elizabeth II uses Windsor Castle at weekends. In addition, she is officially in residence during April and Royal Ascot Week in June.

In November 1992, a fire began in the Queen's Private Chapel and quickly spread, causing extensive damage to the uninsured castle.

This fire played a crucial part in changes to the monarchy. Throughout the year, the royal family had been under siege because of the breakdown in the marriages of **Charles** and **Andrew**. The monarchy was at its lowest ebb with the newspapers full of personal scandals ranging from recorded private telephone conversations to intimate photographs.

When the government offered to pay the £100 million restoration costs from taxation, there was public outrage. What the royal family owned, as opposed to the Crown, was questioned as never before.

It was estimated that the Crown was worth £6.5 billion. But, as the Queen did not pay tax and most of her family received tax-free income, nobody knew where their private finances ended and the Crown's began. Questions were asked about the art collections, the palaces and their expenses, as the royal lifestyle was revealed to be more fitting to a past empire than to an economically depressed nation.

The Queen agreed to changes. She accepted that the Royal Yacht would no longer continue as her private yacht and that the royal trains and planes would no longer be as freely available to members of her family as they had been.

In addition, her family began to pay tax and to receive a greatly reduced Civil List. And **BUCKINGHAM PALACE** was opened to the public to pay for Windsor's restoration.

The Queen continues to be very fond of Windsor and she held her 70th birthday celebrations in the Waterloo Chamber.

ST GEORGE'S CHAPEL

Edward III built St George's Chapel and it was here, in 1348, that he founded the Order of the Garter. The Order, which is the most prestigious in England, consisted only of his family and most favoured subjects. Edward based it on the mythological Knights of the Round Table.

Today there are twenty-four members in addition to those from the royal family: the Queen Mother, Prince Philip, Prince Charles and the Duke of Kent.

The annual service is held in the chapel each June and the motto of the Order is: 'honi soit qui mal y pense', interpreted as 'Evil be to him who evil thinks'.

The Prince of Wales (later **Edward VII**) married Princess Alexandra of Denmark here on 5th March 1863. He wanted a more public wedding, but **Queen Victoria** insisted on the chapel. And even then, his mother refused to participate in the wedding, claiming it was too soon after Albert's death. She would only watch the service from the gallery.

Prince Charles was confirmed in the chapel at Easter 1965. **The Duke of Edinburgh** took no part in the service, preferring to read a book. The Archbishop of Canterbury later called him "bloody rude".

St George's Chapel became the mausoleum for the royal family.

■ **Edward IV** was the first monarch to be buried here in 1483.

■ **Henry VI** was originally buried at Chertsey Abbey in 1471 not far from Windsor. He was known as the 'Holy King' and visits by pilgrims to his tomb became so profitable that **Richard III** brought his body to St George's in 1484 to share in the profits.

■ **Henry VIII** was buried here even though he disliked Windsor. He lies next to his third wife, Jane Seymour, who died after giving birth to **Edward VI**.

■ **Charles I** was refused a place at **WESTMINSTER ABBEY** and his body was hastily interred at Windsor in the tomb of Henry VIII.

■ The Hanoverian kings, **George I, George III, George IV** and **William IV** were all buried here. George II was buried at **WESTMINSTER ABBEY**.

■ **Edward VII**

■ **George V**

■ **George VI**

AROUND THE TOWN

2 | Windsor Station

Queen Victoria had the railway line extended from Slough to Windsor in 1849 so that she could get to the castle by train.

An assassination attempt was made on the queen by Roderick MacLean here. He was tried for treason but was found insane and sent to a mental hospital.

3 | Church Street

Nell Gwynne stayed in a house in Church Street, next door to the Old King's Head tea room, when **Charles II** visited Windsor. It is rumoured that there was a tunnel running from her house to the castle.

4 | 2 Curfew Yard off Thames Street
In this house in 1648, Oliver Cromwell signed the death warrant of **Charles I**.

5 | Hodgkiss & Sons St Leonards Road
These fishmongers supply Windsor Castle.

ROYAL RESIDENCES IN AND AROUND THE GREAT PARK
6 | FROGMORE HOUSE & MAUSOLEUM
Tel. (01753) 868286
Open May & August
Admission charge
Frogmore House was built in the 1680s and was for many years leased to George Fitzroy, the illegitimate son of **Charles II** and Barbara Villiers.

In 1792, **George III**'s wife, Charlotte, used the house whilst her husband was confined at Windsor for the last years of his life.

After her death in 1818, Frogmore passed to her daughter, Princess Augusta. When **Queen Victoria** came to the throne in 1837, it was given to her mother, the Duchess of Kent.

Victoria's grandson (later **George V**) lived at Frogmore for several years before he became king.

FROGMORE
MAUSOLEUM

FROGMORE MAUSOLEUM
The mausoleum was built by **Queen Victoria** as a burial place for **Prince Albert**. It cost £200,000, just under the price of the rebuilding of **OSBORNE HOUSE**. When Victoria died in 1901, her body was buried next to Albert's.

In 1972 the Duke of Windsor (the abdicated **Edward VIII**) was given a royal funeral at Frogmore after his four decades in exile. Frogmore lies a short distance from Fort Belvedere, the home he had loved so much as Prince of Wales. Wallis Simpson, the Duchess of Windsor, is buried beside him.

The mausoleum is also the burial place for privileged members of the Royal Household, for example, Patrick Plunket, once Master of the Royal Household and a close friend of **Elizabeth II**. The Queen herself designed the effigy for his tombstone.

7 | ROYAL LODGE
Private

Built for the Prince Regent (later **George IV)** by Sir Jeffrey Wyattville. The Royal Lodge has been the weekend home of **the Queen Mother** since her marriage to **George VI** in 1925. When they moved in, there were many Victorian alterations and they renovated the house to its original design.

The Queen Mother and **Princess Margaret** spend most of their free weekends at the Lodge.

Royal lodge given as permanent home to Prince Andrew 2002

8 | CUMBERLAND LODGE
Private

Cumberland Lodge was home to the Duke of Cumberland, the son of **George II**.

He led the English army against the Scottish army of 'Bonny' Prince Charlie in 1745 and became known as 'the butcher of Culloden'.

The duke was made ranger of the Great Park and was responsible for the setting out of the lakes at Virginia Water.

As a girl, **Queen Victoria** stayed at Cumberland Lodge when she came to visit her uncle, **William IV**, at Windsor Castle.

9 | FORT BELVEDERE
Private

The Prince of Wales (later **Edward VIII**) bought the eighteenth century mock castle in 1930 after leasing it for a few years.

Freda Dudley Ward was his mistress at the time and supervised the extensive modernisation of the house including the addition of a swimming pool.

The house was famous during the 1920s and early 1930s for many parties which the prince held. The Fort was also a sanctuary where he could meet with Wallis Simpson during the early years of their relationship.

On 10th December 1936, as king, he signed the abdication papers in the octagonal drawing room overlooking the pool. The following day he left Fort Belvedere and went into exile with twice divorced Wallis Simpson.

He was given the title Duke of Windsor and they married on 3rd June 1937 at Chateau Conde, Monts, near Tours. Edward died in Paris on 28th May 1972.

10 | CRANBOURNE TOWER near Cranbourne Gate

Charles II built a hunting lodge here in the 1670s. The red brick tower is all that remains.

11 | SUNNINGHILL PARK HOUSE off B383
Private

Home to the Queen's second son, **Prince Andrew**.

Sunninghill Park stands on the site of an old mansion given by **George VI** in 1947 to Princess Elizabeth on her marriage to Prince Philip. But a fire destroyed the property before they could move in. They intended to rebuild, but this became unnecessary when, on the death of her father, Elizabeth became Queen.

The site stood empty for forty years until she gave it to Prince Andrew on his marriage to Sarah Ferguson in 1986.

They spent £5 million designing the present house which the media named 'South Fork', a pun on his recently given title, Duke of York, and the homestead featured in the American TV series 'Dallas'.

Since their divorce, Andrew has lived at the house alone. He has a desk-job at the Ministry of Defence in Whitehall and lives at **BUCKINGHAM PALACE** during the week.

In February 1997, Sarah announced that she was going to move back temporarily into Sunninghill Park as part of her attempt to curb spending. She had been renting Kingsbourne House, in Virginia Water, for £2000 per week.

12 | CASTLEWOOD HOUSE Egham, Surrey
Private

[handwritten annotation: Relinquished 2002 when Prince Andrew moved to Royal Lodge, without Sarah, who now lives in Windlesham village]

The Duke and Duchess of York rented Castlewood House during the construction of Sunninghill Park. Castlewood is owned by King Hussein of Jordan.

13 | SWINLEY FOREST GOLF CLUB
Private Golf Club

Since his divorce, **Prince Andrew** has become a golf enthusiast and plays here regularly.

14 | WINDLESHAM MANOR Windlesham, near Bracknell, Surrey
Private

Princess Elizabeth rented Windlesham Manor shortly after her marriage to Prince Philip in 1947. The manor replaced the burnt-down Sunninghill Park as their weekend retreat.

15 | RUNNYMEDE near Old Windsor
Public access at all times

Here in June 1215 **King John** was forced to sign an agreement with his noblemen. Known as the Magna Carta, the agreement set out for the first time to define the powers of the sovereign and the rights of his subjects.

There is a plaque marking the site and one of the copies of the Magna Carta can be seen at the British Museum in London.

RACING AND HORSES

The Queen has an extensive knowledge and love of horses and racing. Amongst the many equestrian events she and the royal family attend are:

16 | THE ROYAL WINDSOR HORSE SHOW Home Park

Horse show held every May.

17 | GUARDS' POLO CLUB Smith's Lawn, Windsor Great Park

Tel. (01784) 437797

Smith's Lawn is home to polo matches every Sunday afternoon.

Prince Charles follows his father as a regular and keen competitor of the sport.

PRINCE CHARLES PLAYING POLO

Sarah, Duchess of York's father, Major Ronald Ferguson, was the Prince's personal polo manager until the scandal of his visits to London massage clubs forced him to resign.

18 | ASCOT RACECOURSE High Street, Ascot
Tel. (01344) 22211
The racecourse was built by **Queen Anne** in 1711.

During the Royal Week in June, the Queen and members of her family arrive at the racecourse by horse-drawn carriage through the Great Park.

They mingle in the Royal Enclosure with vetted members of the public. Until 1955, the purity of royalty was preserved by forbidding divorcees, bankrupts or convicted criminals entry into the Enclosure. Luckily this rule was dropped before the marriages of Princess Margaret, Prince Charles, Princess Anne and Prince Andrew ended in divorce.

19 | WEST ILSLEY near Didcot
Private
The Queen has her horse stables here. Because it is close to Windsor, she is able to make frequent visits.

20 | POLHAMPTON LODGE STUD near Newbury
Private
The Queen breeds race horses here.

SCHOOLS
Since the early 1950s when **Prince Charles** attended prep school in London, it has become customary for members of the royal family to attend school rather than receive private tuition.

Berkshire, due to its proximity to Windsor, has become popular for their education.

21 | HEATHEDOWN PREPARATORY SCHOOL Ascot
Prince Edward went to this preparatory school before going on to **GORDONSTOUN** in Scotland.

22 | EATON END Datchet
The Queen's cousin, the Duke of Kent, sent two of his children, Lady Helen and Lord George Windsor, to this school.

Their home at the time was Coppins, at Iver in Buckinghamshire. The late Victorian house was formerly owned by Princess Victoria, the unmarried daughter of Edward VII. She left Coppins to her nephew, the present Duke's father.

PRINCE WILLIAM'S FIRST DAY AT **ETON COLLEGE**

23 | **ETON COLLEGE** Eton
Eton College was established in 1441 by the twenty-year old **Henry VI**, for seventy 'poor and worthy' scholars. The intention was for them to complete their education at the newly founded **KING'S COLLEGE, CAMBRIDGE.**

Today pupils still wear the back mourning coats, designed to commemorate the death of **George III**.

Prince William, the eldest son of **Prince Charles**, attends the school.

24 | **LINDGROVE PREPARATORY SCHOOL** near Reading
Private
Prince William attended the prep school before starting at **ETON COLLEGE**.

25 | **COOKHAM**
Here on the Thames in July, newly hatched swans are gathered and marked in the ceremony of 'Swan Upping'.

Swans first came to England as a gift to **Richard I** from Queen Beatrice of Cyprus. They were protected as royal birds - highly valued for their meat and decorative feathers.

All swans on the Thames are owned either by the Queen, or two of the ancient City of London livery companies. The Queen's swans are left unmarked, whilst the others have marks cut into their beaks.

Oxfordshire

1 | OXFORD

Tourist Information: tel. (01865) 726871

Oxford's royal connections go back to the twelfth century when **Henry II** built Beaumont Palace. His sons, the future kings **Richard I** and **John**, were born there.

The university began after 1167 when students gathered after Henry ordered their return from continental universities. The king's decree was to show his anger at France for allowing sanctuary to Archbishop Thomas Becket, his troublesome ex-chancellor.

Henry II is therefore known as the 'father' of British Universities.

Christchurch College St Aldgates

Charles I lived here for three years at the start of the Civil War in 1642 and established a Royal Mint in the college buildings.

In 1859 the Prince of Wales (later **Edward VII**) spent three terms at Christchurch. His father, **Prince Albert**, wanted to instil discipline and so he was educated in isolation from other students. He lived outside the college, at Frewin Hall and was seen only by his tutors and equerries.

Not surprisingly Edward seized his earliest opportunity to escape Oxford by joining the army in Ireland.

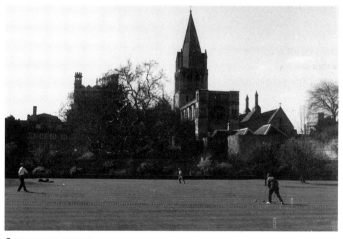

CHRISTCHURCH COLLEGE

Magdalen College High Street

The Prince of Wales (later **Edward VIII**) was educated here after leaving Dartmouth Naval College.

In contrast to his grandfather, Edward was allowed to socialise and to hold parties without restriction. Throughout his life he regarded Oxford with great affection.

BLENHEIM PALACE

2 | **BLENHEIM PALACE** Woodstock

Tel. (01993) 811274

Open March-Oct: daily 10.30am-5.30pm (park open all year)

Admission charge

Blenheim Palace stands in the Royal Manor of Woodstock and was built on the site of a royal hunting lodge.

Henry I enclosed the land for his collection of exotic animals. Since then, other monarchs have used it:

■ **Henry II** built a home in the park and surrounded it by a maze for Rosamund Clifford, his mistress. Rosamund is buried at nearby *Godstow Abbey Church*.

■ **Elizabeth I** was imprisoned here for eleven months during the reign of her sister, **Mary I**. It was one of many houses she spent time in during the turbulent power struggles between Catholics and Protestants.

■ **James I** used Woodstock as a hunting park, much to the annoyance of his councillors, who hated coming to the small lodge with the consequent shortage of facilities.

During the **Civil War**, the house was damaged and only the gatehouse remained.

In 1704 **Queen Anne** gave Woodstock to John Churchill, the Duke of Marlborough, as a reward for his victory over the French at Blenheim.

As a favourite of the queen, Marlborough's wife, Sarah, was able to obtain enough finance to build Blenheim Palace as one of the most magnificent private houses in Britain. However, the remains of the old manor were pulled down to enhance the view.

Avon

1 | **BADMINTON HOUSE** Great Badminton
Private
Tel. (01454) 218272
Until the death of the Duke of Beaufort, members of the royal family stayed at Badminton House during the horse trials in May and when attending the Cheltenham Races in March.

George V's wife, Queen Mary, loved Badminton House and was a frequent visitor during the Second World War.

Gloucestershire

This area is home to the Queen's two eldest children, Prince Charles and Princess Anne. Many cousins and friends also live here.

Prince Charles is a keen hunter and hunts frequently with both the Quorn and Belvoir Hunts.

2 | **HIGHGROVE HOUSE** Tetbury, near Doughton
Private
Home of **Prince Charles**.

The house was originally built in 1796, but much redesigned in 1894 after a fire. In 1981, at the time of his marriage to **Diana**, Charles bought Highgrove and has now restored the house to its original design.

He was attracted to the house by its relative simplicity and modesty. But because of its size, staff and guests often stay at the local hotel.

In addition, there was great potential to develop the gardens. Charles has succeeded in this and has created one of the great gardens of modern times. He continues to spend many hours secluded in his favourite spot, the kitchen garden.

Charles uses Highgrove as a refuge and a place to pursue his interests and ideas. His development of wild flower cultivation, recycling of waste and solar-powered heating have all been put into action at Highgrove.

The thousand acre estate has been given over to natural farming and is today one of Britain's leading organic farms. Products from the estate are sold widely under the name, 'Duchy Original'.

3 | **GATCOMBE PARK** near Minchinhampton
Private
(grounds open Aug for horse trials)
Elizabeth II bought the Gatcombe Park Estate for **Princess Anne** in 1976 following her marriage to Mark Philips.

Since their divorce, Anne lives in the main house with her children, Zara and Peter, and her second husband, Tim Lawrence.

Philips manages the estate, where he lives in a farmhouse.

As Olympic equestrians, Princess Anne and Mark Philips created a horse trials course known as the Gatcombe Park Horse Trials, which they continue to host each year. In addition, Philips runs the equestrian centre at the Gleneagles Hotel in Scotland.

4 | NETHER LYPIATT MANOR Bisley
Private
The country home of the Queen's cousin, Prince Michael of Kent.

In London they reside at Kensington Palace. Princess Michael has started a career as a writer. Prince Michael is a keen motorist and participates in the London to Brighton Classic Car Run each November.

5 | CIRENCESTER PARK Cirencester
Private
Tel. (01285) 653225
Prince Charles regularly plays polo during the season, which begins here in April.

6 | BERKELEY CASTLE Berkeley, near Dursley
Tel. (01453) 810332
Open April: Tue-Sun 2.00-5.00pm; May-Sept: Tue-Sat 11.00am-5.00pm & Sun 2.00-5.00pm; Oct: Sun 2.00-4.30pm
Admission charge
Edward II was killed at Berkeley Castle on the orders of his estranged wife, Isabella, known as 'the She-Wolf'. After his death, she was imprisoned at **CASTLE RISING** in Norfolk. (See **CASTLE RISING** for full story.)

Edward is buried at *Gloucester Abbey* - surprisingly with Isabella's heart.

Worcestershire

7 | WORCESTER CATHEDRAL Worcester
Tel. (01905) 28854
Open daily 7.30am-6.30pm
After his death at Newark, **King John** was buried under the high altar of the cathedral.

His successor, **Henry III**, was imprisoned here after defeat at the Battle of Lewes in 1264. The king was fighting Simon de Montfort, his brother-in-law, who led an army of rebels. In 1265, they forced the king to convene a parliament, but lost at the battle of Evesham later that year.

8 | BATTLE OF WORCESTER The Commandery, Sidbury, Worcester
Tel. (01905) 355071
Open daily 10am-5pm (closed Sun am)
Charles II's headquarters at the Battle of Worcester during the Civil War.

After his father's execution in 1649 during the Civil War, his son Charles proclaimed himself King but was only crowned in Scotland.

The twenty-one year old led a Royalist army against Cromwell and the Parliamentarians. He lost at the Battle of Worcester on 3rd September 1651 and escaped to Boscobel Wood, outside Telford, Shropshire. Here, he famously hid in an oak tree before travelling to France via Bristol, disguised as a servant.

Warwickshire

9 | KENILWORTH CASTLE
Tel. (01926) 52078
Open daily 10am-6pm (Oct-March: Tue-Sun 10am-4pm)
Admission charge
Kenilworth was the home of Simon de Montfort who fought against **Henry III** in the thirteenth century. (See **Worcester Cathedral** above.) The castle was captured by the royalists after the Battle of Evesham which saw the defeat of de Montfort.

Henry IV was the first to use the castle as a royal residence. It was little used and in 1543 **Elizabeth I** gave Kenilworth to her favourite courtier, the Earl of Leicester.

The castle was ruined during the Civil War.

Northamptonshire

10 | ALTHORP HALL Great Brington
Tel. (01604) 770107
Family home of **Diana, Princess of Wales**.

The Spencer family fortune was founded on sheep farming and in 1508 they built Althorp Hall. The house was redesigned in 1786.

Diana's father inherited the Earldom of Spencer when she was fourteen and they moved from the **Sandringham** estate to Althorp.

Diana first met **Prince Charles** here when he was a guest of her elder sister, Sarah.

Leicestershire

11 | BATTLE OF BOSWORTH FIELD Market Bosworth
Open April-Oct: daily 11am-5pm
Admission charge
Richard III was killed by the future **Henry VII** at this battle in 1485, which ended the War of the Roses.

Nottinghamshire

12 | NEWARK CASTLE Newark
Tel. (01636) 611 908
King John died here on 18th October 1216 from dysentery whilst fighting the Barons' Wars. The king had failed to keep to the terms of the Magna Carta signed at **Runnymede** in Berkshire and so the Crown was offered by the Barons to Prince Louis of France. Louis arrived in England and a civil war ensued. John lost most of the south-east but kept the Midlands region. His son, **Henry III**, defeated the Barons during his reign.

The castle was destroyed during the Civil War of the seventeenth century, leaving only ruins.

East Anglia

SANDRINGHAM HOUSE

1 | **SANDRINGHAM HOUSE** near Dersingham, Norfolk
Tel. Buckingham Palace for details (0171) 930 4832
Open Easter-Sept: daily 11.00am-4.45pm (when Queen not in residence)
Admission charge
Queen Victoria's heir (later **Edward VII**) needed a country residence.

The Prince of Wales disliked the formality of **BALMORAL** and **OSBORNE**. His father, **Prince Albert**, suggested he invest in his own property and by 1861, Edward had saved £220,000 from his official income to purchase the estate.

The house was rebuilt in an Elizabethan style, but with modern features, such as an American bowling alley. New wings were added for staff and guests and the extensive grounds were remodelled with lakes.

Edward loved Sandringham and spent as much time here as possible, often from Christmas to the end of February. His main pleasure was shooting and he had the clocks put forward by half an hour to maximise daylight. This became known as 'Sandringham Time'.

Though the prince was expected to attend the estate's church, *St Mary Margaret*, he did not enjoy it. Often he would arrive half way through the service and demand a short sermon.

On Sunday afternoons, Edward took great pride in walking around his estate. He thought himself an ideal landlord and indeed, was appointed to the 'Royal Commission on Working Class Housing' because the workers' cottages were considered model dwellings.

As Prince of Wales, Edward led fashionable society and this moved with him to Sandringham, causing havoc until the rural roads of East Anglia were upgraded.

In May 1910, **Edward VII** died at Sandringham after a series of heart attacks brought on by bronchitis. The king had been a lifetime smoker with a daily consumption of twelve Cuban cigars and at least two packets of full-strength cigarettes.

His widow, Queen Alexandra, refused to move out of the house forcing their son, now **George V**, to stay at **YORK COTTAGE** in the grounds until her death in 1926.

George V's fondness for Sandringham was as much for the peace and quiet as it was for its association with his father's memory.

In 1932 George began the tradition of Christmas broadcasts from the house. The first was made from a tiny room under the main stairs.

He died at Sandringham on 20th January 1936. On his death bed, he was asked if he wished to be moved to Bognor, the Sussex seaside town where he had previously convalesced after an illness. His last words were, 'Bugger Bognor'.

George VI came to the throne in 1936 after the abdication of his brother, **Edward VIII**. The shy and intensely private king found solace on the estate. He suffered from an inhibiting stammer and he undertook extensive speech therapy here.

At Sandringham, he followed the lifestyle of his father and grandfather. Indeed, the day before his death from lung cancer, he still managed to go shooting. He died at the house on 6th February 1952.

His daughter has used Sandringham regularly since she became queen. One of the Edwardian wings has been demolished and the atmosphere is now more homely. Guests are placed in estate houses, such as Anmer Hall and **YORK COTTAGE**, leaving the main house free for immediate family.

Sandringham is the Queen's private home and does not belong to the Crown. Apart from Government papers, state affairs never intrude and the house is used solely for family and friends. Indeed, in 1996 her grandson and future heir, **Prince William**, preferred the privacy of the estate to the publicity of a skiing trip with his father.

Their pursuits remain the same as when the house was first built: shooting, riding and family gatherings.

At Christmas, the royal family attend St Mary Margaret's and receive gifts from members of the public.

Houses on the estate:
YORK COTTAGE
George V used the house from 1893 as Duke of York and as king until 1926.

He enjoyed its lack of pretension although his friends described it as: "a suburban villa more suitable for a modest solicitor than for a royal family of eight with servants".

He spent his time gardening and building his large stamp collection. This, by the time of his death, consisted of a quarter of a million stamps spread over 325 volumes. The Queen continues the collection and it is now the largest in the world.

George VI was born at York Cottage on 14th December 1895, a date of particular significance for his great-grandmother, **Queen Victoria**, because it was the anniversary of Prince Albert's death.

PARK HOUSE

Edward VII built this as a ten-bedroom guest house.

Park House was the home of **Diana Spencer** who lived here whilst her father was an equerry to the Queen. They moved to **ALTHORP HALL** when she was fourteen and he inherited the earldom.

Despite the breakdown of her parents' marriage, Diana preferred living here to the vast spaces of **ALTHORP**. Whilst at Park House, Diana attended *Sillfield School* in the nearby village of Wymondham. After this she went to *Riddlesworth Hall*, also in Norfolk, where she won two prizes: one for looking after the school hamster and the second for helpfulness.

Park House is now a home for the disabled.

2 | CASTLE RISING near Kings Lynn, Norfolk

Tel. (01553) 631330
Open daily 10am-6pm (Oct-March: Wed-Sun 10am-4pm)
Admission charge

Edward II's widow, Queen Isabella, died at this Norman castle in 1358. Isabella had been banished here by her son, **Edward III**, for the last 28 years of her life.

Edward II had been a weak king and Isabella, known as the 'She-Wolf', was jealous of his homosexual love for Piers Gaveston. In January 1327 he abdicated and was held at **BERKELEY CASTLE** in Gloucestershire. In September Isabella arranged Edward's murder. She then imprisoned their son in the **TOWER OF LONDON** and ruled with her lover, Roger Mortimer.

When the boy came of age as **Edward III**, he executed Mortimer and banished his mother to Castle Rising.

After Isabella's death, she was buried at **CHRIST CHURCH GREYFRIARS** in the City of London. However, her heart was taken to Gloucester Cathedral where it was placed in the tomb of her husband.

3 | NEWMARKET RACECOURSE

Tel. (01638) 663482
July course: Cambridge Road, Newmarket
Rowley Mile course: off Hamilton Road, Newmarket

Since it was built, Newmarket Racecourse has been a royal favourite.

Charles II had a house nearby, long-since demolished. He used it when he came to the races, often with his illegitimate son, the Duke of Monmouth, and his brother, the Duke of York (later **James II**).

Once at the Newmarket races, Monmouth bet all his remaining money on the prophecy of Charles's Indian astrologer. Much to the king's amusement, the horse finished way down the field, leaving his son destitute.

Edward VII had stables just outside the town, at Egerton House. His old friend and former mistress, Lily Langtry, lived nearby at Regal Lodge in Kentford.

4 | CAMBRIDGE

Tourist Information (01223) 322640

This ancient university town has had many royal connections.

   Henry VI was the first of several monarchs to found a college, when he established Kings College in 1441.

   The Duke of Edinburgh is chancellor of the university. When visiting, he stays at *5 Latham Road*, on the edge of the city. The house is home to the vice-chancellor but a flat is kept available for the duke.

TRINITY COLLEGE

Trinity College Trinity Street

The Prince of Wales (later **Edward VII**) spent a short while here and lived in isolation at *Madingley Hall*, west of Cambridge.

   Prince Albert (later **George VI**) came to Trinity for a year after the First World War had finished. He left in 1920 to carry out royal duties, as he was to be made Duke of York. The prince lived with his brother, the Duke of Gloucester, at *Southacre, Latham Road*, during his year at the college.

   Prince Charles was the first member of the royal family to obtain a degree. He received a respectable 2.ii class degree in Anthropology from Trinity. He lived in rooms on the second floor of the *New Court* before moving to the south side of *Great Court*.

   In his second year, the college Master allowed Charles to use his rooms as a meeting place with his first girlfriend. She was Lucia Santa Cruz, daughter of the Chilean Ambassador, and three years older. Charles is now godfather to one of her children.

Jesus College Jesus Lane
Prince Edward spent three years here from 1983-86.

He studied Archaeology and Anthropology but much of his free time was taken up with acting at the university's *ADC Theatre*.

AUDLEY END HOUSE

5 | AUDLEY END HOUSE near Saffron Walden, Essex
Tel. (01799) 522399
Open April-Oct: Wed-Sun 12-6pm (grounds open at 10am)
Admission charge
Charles II used Audley End as a country residence after his return from exile in France.

The Jacobean mansion had been built by the family of the Earl of Suffolk at a cost of £190,000. This, along with the upkeep of the house, threatened to bankrupt the earl.

Charles's low purchase offer of £50,000 was therefore accepted. Unfortunately, the years of the Commonwealth had stripped the monarchy of its wealth and Charles was unable to provide the money. However he did pay for the upkeep and a small rent.

Every spring and autumn, the Court came to Audley End so that Whitehall could be "cleaned out and put in repair". The king swapped theatregoing and the games of tennis, pell-mell, bowls and cockfighting for a country life of hare-coursing, hunting, hawking and racing at **NEWMARKET**.

On the king's death in 1685, the house reverted to the Suffolk family.

6 | EPPING FOREST Essex

Information Centre (0181) 508 0028

Public access at all times

Queen Boadicea was defeated in 61AD for the final time by the Romans at the hill fort of Ambursbury Banks.

Boadicea had become leader of the Iceni tribe the previous year on the death of her husband. When the Romans seized tribal lands in Norfolk and Suffolk, she led a rebellion against them.

With other disgruntled tribes, she won a series of victories including the destruction of the Roman stronghold at London.

After her defeat at Epping, she fled with her two daughters and committed suicide. Her grave is rumoured to be at several places, including the sites of Charing Cross and Kings Cross stations.

The last Saxon king, **Harold**, prayed at Waltham Abbey on his way to fight William of Normandy in 1066. He had founded the abbey in 1060 and was brought here for burial after his defeat. The original abbey was destroyed in 1540 during the Dissolution of the Monasteries and a church now stands in its place.

Epping Forest was a favourite hunting forest for the Tudors.

■ **Henry VIII** built a grandstand in 1543, just north of Chingford, from where he could watch the chase.

■ **Elizabeth I** converted it into a hunting lodge and it is now the site of the *Museum of Epping Forest*.

■ **Mary I** was held prisoner at Copt Hall, north of the forest, by her half-brother,

■ **Edward VI**, during his short reign.

During the seventeenth century, highwaymen terrorised the area and the forest fell into disuse. In 1878 it was bought by the Corporation of London to prevent housing development.

7 | HAVERING-ATTE-BOWER CASTLE (demolished)

near Romford, Essex

The castle was officially the royal residence of queens from the time of **Edward the Confessor**.

In the sixteenth century, both **Henry VIII** and **Elizabeth I** used Havering Castle as a hunting lodge.

Elizabeth stayed here in 1588 when the English Fleet were mustered at Tilbury against the Spanish Armada. Two thousand horsemen were stationed at nearby Romford for the queen's protection.

The castle was broken up during the Commonwealth.

Hertfordshire

1 | ASHRIDGE HOUSE Little Gaddesden, near Tring
Private

Queen Mary held her half-sister (later **Elizabeth I**) here in 1554 at the height of the Catholic-Protestant power struggle.

So great was Mary's fear of a Protestant rebellion that she had Elizabeth, though ill, transferred, with an escort of over 250 soldiers, to the TOWER OF LONDON until the danger passed.

2 | BERKHAMPSTED CASTLE Castle Street, Berkhampsted
Tel. (01442) 871737
Open Mon-Sat 9.30am-dusk (Sun 2.00pm-dusk)
Free

Berkhampsted Castle is now in ruins.

A castle was first built here by the Saxons as part of a link of defences guarding the Thames Valley.

William I was offered the Crown of England at the castle, in the winter of 1066, before proceeding to Westminster for his coronation.

Henry II, in the twelfth century, gave the castle to his friend, Thomas Becket, Archbishop of Canterbury. Before their fall-out, the king often stayed here.

In 1320, **Edward II** gave Berkhampsted as one of many gifts to his homosexual lover, Piers Gaveston, who entertained extravagantly at the castle.

Edward III's son, the Black Prince, lived at the castle before his death at the TOWER OF LONDON.

Berkhampsted lost its importance and fell into ruin during Tudor times.

3 | KINGS LANGLEY MANOR HOUSE AND PRIORY
Rudolf Steiner School, Kings Langley
Private

During the plague of 1349, **Edward III** moved his Court here from London.

In 1400, the body of Edward's grandson and heir, **Richard II**, was buried at the priory for fourteen years before reburial at Westminster.

The house fell into disrepair and only a few ruins remain.

4 | HATFIELD HOUSE opposite Hatfield Railway Station
Tel. (01707) 275719
Open Tue-Sat 12.00-4.00pm (Sun 1.00-4.30pm)
Admission charge

Hatfield was originally a Saxon manor. After the Norman Conquest, the manor was used by monarchs during their Royal Progress around the country.

In 1496 the manor was rebuilt as a palace by Cardinal Morton. Because of the stability brought by the Tudors, Hatfield was one of the first grand houses built solely for comfort and without defence.

On the death of Morton, Hatfield became the property of the bishops of Ely until **Henry VIII** took possession of the house for his children, the future monarchs Mary, Elizabeth and Edward.

In 1533, whilst staying here, **Mary** was pronounced illegitimate after Henry had declared his marriage to her mother, Catherine of Aragon, illegal.

Elizabeth I was sitting in the garden at Hatfield, in November 1558 when she was proclaimed Queen on the death of her sister, **Mary**.

She had recently returned from the TOWER OF LONDON where she had been imprisoned as the main rival to Mary's Catholic rule.

Elizabeth's first act was to appoint William Cecil as her Chief Minister during her Council of State in the Great Hall.

During her reign, she used Hatfield as a hunting base, but the monarchy was increasingly centred around the palaces on the Thames.

In the 1600s, **James I** exchanged Hatfield with neighbouring THEOBALDS PARK. This had belonged to Robert Cecil, son of Elizabeth's Chief Minister.

Hatfield House was rebuilt in 1611 by Cecil and of the original building, only the Great Hall remains.

5 | THEOBALDS PARK (destroyed)
Cheshunt

James I fell in love with Theobalds on first arriving in England from his native Scotland. For him, the estate represented the wealth of England and he exchanged HATFIELD HOUSE for Theobalds. It was his favourite residence and he died here of kidney failure, with his son at his bedside, on 27 March 1625.

Charles I rode from Theobalds to London to be proclaimed King at both WHITEHALL and Cheapside. The route by which he entered the City of London was commemorated in the names of the streets on the north side of Holborn: Kingsgate Street, King Street, Kings Road, and Theobalds Road.

During the Commonwealth, Oliver Cromwell ordered Theobalds Park to be demolished and the stone, valued at £8,000, to be sold.

Wales

1 | CAERNARFON CASTLE Gwynedd, North Wales
Tel. (01286) 77617
Open daily 9.30am-6.30pm (Oct-March: closes at 4.00pm)
Admission charge

Until 1283, Wales was a series of independent principalities. Though English kings had always owned land in Wales, they had taken little interest in the region and their estates were heavily poached.

   Edward I was well-educated and ambitious, able to speak French, Latin, Italian and Greek. When he inherited from his father, **Henry III**, he was determined to make his mark and embarked on a series of battles to subjugate the Welsh.

INVESTITURE OF CHARLES AS PRINCE OF WALES AT **CAERNARFON CASTLE** IN 1969

He built a string of castles known as the Iron Ring, that included Conwy, Beaumaris, Harlech and Flint. All still stand today.

However, the grandest castle was at Caernarfon, with it fortifications based on those Edward had seen in the Middle East during the crusades.

His son (later **Edward II**) was born here in 1284. In 1301, the young prince was made Prince of Wales both to confirm him as heir and to include Wales in the monarchy.

The investiture of the Prince of Wales did not become a significant ceremony until that of the future **Edward VIII** at the castle in 1911.

Prince Charles was invested here in 1969 at the age of twenty-one. Before the ceremony, Charles spent some time at the University College of Wales at Aberystwyth studying Welsh. On the morning of the investiture, two Welsh Nationalist protesters blew themselves up whilst placing a bomb on a bridge near the castle gates.

Just outside Caernarfon is the gold mine of Clogau St David, where the nugget was found for the wedding rings of the Queen Mother, the Queen, Princess Margaret, Princess Anne and Diana.

2 | HARLECH CASTLE Gwynedd, North Wales
Tel. (01766) 780552
Open daily 9.30am-6.30pm (Oct-March: closes at 4.00pm)
Admission charge
In 1404, the castle fell to the Welsh prince, Owen Glendower, who then held the stronghold for four years before it was returned to the English.

During the Wars of the Roses between the dynasties of York and Lancaster, the Welsh nationalist, Dafydd ab Ieuan ap Einion, took the castle. The Lancastrian **Henry VI**'s wife, Margaret of Anjou, stayed at the castle for safety. Dafydd held Harlech in support of the Lancastrians until defeated by the Yorkist **Edward IV**.

The Welsh national song, 'Men of Harlech', was composed to celebrate Dafydd.

Scotland

The Crown of Scotland united with England in 1603 when **James VI** of Scotland became **James I** of England and the first monarch to rule over the two countries.

James succeeded to the English throne on the death of **Elizabeth I**. As the son of Mary Queen of Scots and Lord Darnley, he was a descendent, through both parents, of **Henry VII**'s daughter, Margaret.

1 | THE PALACE OF HOLYROODHOUSE Edinburgh, Lothian
Tel. (0131) 556 7371
Open daily 9.30am-6.00pm (Nov-March: closes at 4.30pm)
Admission charge
Holyroodhouse is named in memory of St Margaret, mother of **David I**, who brought a fragment of the Holy Rood (Holy Cross) to Scotland. David founded an abbey here in the twelfth century, after his vision of a stag carrying the Cross between its antlers. This became the emblem of the palace.

Many Scottish monarchs preferred the comfort of Holyroodhouse to the bleakness of **EDINBURGH CASTLE**. Today it is the official residence of the Sovereign in Scotland.

THE HISTORY
■ **James II** of Scotland was born here in 1430. He also married and was buried in the abbey. He died from an exploding canon whilst besieging the English at Roxburgh in 1460.
■ **James IV** converted the abbey into a palace and married Margaret Tudor, the eldest daughter of **Henry VII** of England, in the chapel.
■ **Mary Queen of Scots** rebuilt the palace in 1560 and married her cousin, Lord Darnley, here on the 29th July 1565. Their son became **James VI** of Scotland (also **James I** of England).

On the 9th March 1566, Mary's secretary, David Rizzio, was murdered whilst dining in the queen's bedroom. Rizzio was stabbed 56 times on Darnley's orders. The reason was that he had advised Mary against giving Darnley independent royal status.

Later Darnley was himself murdered and on 15th May 1567, Mary married his alleged killer, the Earl of Bothwell, at Holyroodhouse.

In June, she was sent to prison at *Lochleven Castle* on an island in Loch Leven, Kinross, for Darnley's murder. She escaped in 1568.
■ **James VI** was the last king to live here, for as James I he moved his court to England. This was not just because of its greater wealth, but also because the monarchy played a more central and powerful role. In Scotland, the monarch was considered, by the nobility, not much more than the first amongst equals.
■ **Charles II** rebuilt the palace, but never stayed here.
■ During the Jacobite Rebellion, 'Bonny' Prince Charlie (grandson of the last English Stuart King, **James II**) held a ball at Holyroodhouse in 1745 to celebrate the short-lived success of his army.
■ The palace was next used by King Louis XVI of France after great debts had forced him to flee his country.

- **Queen Victoria** refurbished Holyroodhouse as a royal residence. Formerly visiting British monarchs had stayed at *Dalkeith House* in the city centre, home of the Dukes of Buccleuch.
- **George V** and **Queen Mary** restored the interiors of the house.

THE TWENTIETH CENTURY

Elizabeth II visits Edinburgh, at the end of June or beginning of July. She uses Holyroodhouse as a base from which she can visit friends in the area: for example, the Duke of Roxburgh at *Floors Castle*, Kelso. Floors Castle was where **Prince Andrew** proposed to **Sarah Ferguson** in 1985.

At Holyroodhouse, the Queen's official functions include garden parties, investitures and state affairs. In addition she attends the annual service at *St Giles' Cathedral* for the Order of the Thistle, Scotland's highest honour.

There are sixteen members of the Order in addition to those from the royal family: Queen Mother, Duke of Edinburgh, Prince Charles and Princess Anne.

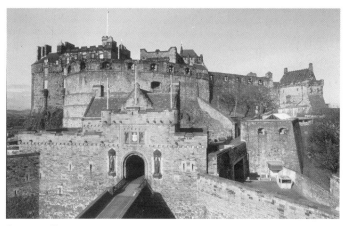

Edinburgh Castle

2 | EDINBURGH CASTLE Castle Rock, Edinburgh, Lothian
Tel. (0131) 244 3101/668 8800
Open daily 9.30am-6.00pm (Nov-March: closes at 5.00pm)
Admission charge
Edinburgh Castle has served as treasury, palace, barracks, arsenal, prison and refuge for Scottish monarchs. It stands on an extinct volcano. The first castle was built here by King Edwin of Northumbria in the seventh century.

- **Malcolm III** rebuilt the castle in the eleventh century and the only surviving part of this is the Chapel of St Margaret built in 1066 by his wife. Margaret died here on hearing news that her husband and son had both died at the battle of Alnwick. She is buried at Dunfermline Abbey.
- In 1124 **David I** moved the capital of Scotland from Dunfermline to Edinburgh and the castle took on a greater status.
- In 1313 **Robert the Bruce** captured the castle from the English invaders and destroyed everything except the chapel.
- **James IV** built the Great Hall in the sixteenth century.

■ In 1566, **Mary Queen of Scots** gave birth to the future **James VI** in the castle, rather than at **HOLYROODHOUSE PALACE**, because of its greater security. But when king, James found the castle dark, depressing and damp and moved to **HOLYROODHOUSE**.

Today it is the location for the Edinburgh tattoo during the city's annual festival in August.

3 | LINLITHGOW PALACE outside Edinburgh, Lothian
Tourist information (0131) 5571700
Open daily 9.30am-6.30pm (not Sun am & Oct-March: closes at 4.30pm)
Admission charge
Linlithgow first became a royal manor in 1139. It was a residence for Scottish monarchs until the Union with England. **Mary, Queen of Scots** was born at Linlithgow in 1542.

The palace was burnt by the English after the Young Pretender, 'Bonny' Prince Charles, visited in 1745 before his defeat at Culloden.

4 | STIRLING CASTLE Stirling, Central Scotland
Tel. (01786) 450000
Open daily 9.30am-6.00pm (Oct-March: closes at 5.00pm)
Admission charge
The present castle dates from the fifteenth century and was built on the site of a previous fortress.

The first castle was held by the English king **Edward I** for many years whilst fighting **Robert the Bruce**. Stirling was finally restored to the Scots in 1347.

It became the favourite of the Stuart monarchs: Mary Stuart was only a month old when she was crowned Queen of Scotland in 1543 in the castle's Chapel of the Holy Rood. And her son **James VI** was crowned king here in 1567 when only a year old.

When he inherited the crown of England, James abandoned plans to rebuild Stirling Castle and moved south.

5 | DUNFERMLINE ABBEY Dunfermline, Fife
Tel. (01383) 724586
Open daily 9.30am-6.30pm (not Sun am & Oct-March: closed Fri)
Admission charge
Dunfermline was the capital of Scotland for over six hundred years. And the English **Edward I** (known at 'the Hammer of the Scots') held court here after his victories in Scotland in the last years of the thirteenth century.

Charles I was born at the palace in 1600 and the last royal resident at Dunfermline was his son (later **Charles II**) in July 1650, the prince stayed here before fighting the Battle of Pitreavie at which he won the Scots over to his side.

Many Scottish monarchs are buried at the abbey, once part of the palace. These include **Malcolm III**, his wife **Margaret**, **David I** and **Robert the Bruce**.

6 | FALKLAND PALACE Falkland, Fife
Tel. (01337) 857397
Open April-Oct: daily 11.00am-5.30pm (closed Sun am)

Admission charge

James V built the palace in the early sixteenth century. He lacked the funds for its upkeep and it soon fell into disrepair.

James died here in 1542 and his daughter Mary, born only the week before at **LINLITHGOW**, became Queen. Mary remained fond of the palace and often stayed between 1561-65, enjoying the hunting in the surrounding countryside.

7 | SCONE PALACE near Perth, Tayside

Tel. (01738) 552300

Open Easter-Oct: Mon-Sat 9.30am-5.00pm (closed Sun am)

Admission charge

This palace was the place of coronation for Scottish kings. It was also the site of the first Scottish parliament in 906AD.

The *Stone of Scone* was taken to **WESTMINSTER ABBEY** in the thirteenth century by **Edward I**.

The last coronation here was that of **Charles II** as king of Scotland, on 1st January 1651, shortly before he lost to Oliver Cromwell at Worcester during the Civil War in England and was forced to flee to France.

8 | GLAMIS CASTLE Glamis, near Forfar, Tayside

Tel. (01307) 840 242

Open April-Oct: daily 10.30am-5.30pm

Admission charge

Glamis is the ancestral home of the Earl of Strathmore and Kinghorn.

■ **Malcolm III** is said to have died here. Earlier, in 1057, he defeated and killed **Macbeth**, whose ghost supposedly haunts the castle.
■ The castle was forfeited to the crown during the reign of **James V**. The 7th Earl was imprisoned at Edinburgh for witchcraft and plotting the death of the king. Glamis returned to the earl after James's death.

The youngest daughter of the 14th Earl of Strathmore was Elizabeth Bowes-Lyon (later **the Queen Mother**). She spent much of her childhood at the castle.

After her marriage to the Duke of York (later **George VI**), they spent part of their honeymoon here.

Their second daughter, **Princess Margaret**, was born at Glamis in 1930. Margaret was the first member of the immediate royal family to be born in Scotland for over three hundred years.

9 | BALMORAL near Crathie, Grampians

Tel. (013397) 423345

Gardens open May-July: Mon-Sat 10am-5pm

Admission charge

Balmoral has been the royal family's private Scottish home since Victoria's reign. The name comes from the Gaelic word for 'majestic dwelling': Bouchmorale.

Queen Victoria and **Prince Albert** bought the property in 1852, after renting it for several years. They were particularly drawn to the area as it reminded Albert of his homeland and so rebuilt the house in granite as a German baronial castle.

Balmoral is a sporting estate of 17,000 acres around the River Dee, with shooting, fishing and deer-stalking as major attractions.

Victoria's fondness for Scotland restored pride to the country after the long years of depression following the Jacobite defeat in 1745. Scottish culture became fashionable again and laws banning the wearing of kilts were rescinded.

Queen Victoria created the Victoria and the Balmoral tartans for the interior of the castle. She enjoyed her role as local laird, frequently visiting her tenants and even inviting them to the wedding of the Prince of Wales at **WINDSOR CASTLE**.

Victoria was increasingly drawn to Balmoral after Albert's death in 1861, spending up to five months a year at the castle until her own death in 1901.

THE QUEEN RECEIVING
FLOWERS AT THE
BRAEMAR GAMES

THE TWENTIETH CENTURY

The royal family have always enjoyed good relations with the locals. There has however been the occasional hiccup: **Edward VIII** held a house party at Balmoral in August 1936, with Mrs Simpson as the hostess.

This caused much gossip. But what most annoyed them was his refusal to open a new hospital, claiming to be in mourning for the recent death of his father.

Still, all would have been well if Edward had not been seen that day at the station, casually dressed to collect his divorced mistress. A scandal ensued.

George VI was fond of Balmoral. A modest family man, he far preferred the life of a country gentleman to that of a king.

It was at Balmoral that Prince Philip of Greece proposed to Princess Elizabeth in 1947. She accepted on the king's condition that Philip's name be changed from Schleswig-Holstein-Sonderburg-Glucksburg to something English. Philip chose Mountbatten, the anglicised version of his mother's German name, Battenburg.

Elizabeth II arrives at Balmoral on the 14th August each year for a month's stay.

In September, she hosts the Gillies Ball at the castle [a gillie is a hunting servant]. She also attends the Braemar Games, at *Braemar Castle*, the site of **Malcolm III**'s eleventh century hunting lodge.

However, it is not all holiday, as during her stay, the Queen receives an annual visit from the Prime Minister.

TROUBLES IN THE FIRM

The royal family call themselves 'The Firm' and each year, at Balmoral, they review the past year and their future plans.

In 1992, these discussions were dominated by the marital troubles of **Prince Charles** and **Prince Andrew**. Tape recordings of Charles and Diana's separate intimate phone conversations had been published in the press.

But worst of all were photographs taken of Andrew's wife. These were first revealed to them when newspapers showed Sarah topless and cavorting in the South of France with her 'financial adviser', John Bryan. To their added horror, the Queen's two granddaughters were in the photographs, looking on.

BIRKHALL HOUSE

The Prince of Wales (later **Edward VII**) was given this house on the Balmoral estate when he married in 1863.

Edward disliked the gloom of Balmoral during his mother's long widowhood and soon moved to nearby *Abergeldie Castle*, which he leased from the Gordon Family.

Birkhall was then used as a guest house before it became home to **the Queen Mother** who stays here when the royal family visits Balmoral.

Given to Prince Charles 2002

10 | GORDONSTOUN SCHOOL Duffus, near Elgin, Grampian
Private

Prince Philip was sent here in the 1930s. Its philosophy is based upon self-reliance and love of the outdoors.

Philip chose to break the royal tradition of private tuition and sent all three sons to the school.

Other royals have attended, including Princess Anne's son, Peter Philips.

11 | CASTLE OF MEY Thurso, Highlands
Private

The Queen Mother bought the semi-ruined Castle of Mey after the death of her husband, **George VI**.

She restored Mey and added 120 acres of mixed farm land, where a prized herd of Aberdeen Angus cattle are bred.

Mey is used during the months of August and October, when hunting and fishing are at their best. The castle has its own trout ponds and deer park.

The royal family visits the castle during their annual cruise around the Western Isles to Aberdeen in August. The Royal Yacht drops anchor at the nearby port of Scrabster and they picnic with the Queen Mother before departing under a firework display on the castle walls.

12 | IONA ABBEY Isle of Iona, near Isle of Mull, Western Isles
Open daily
Free

St Columba built a monastery on this island in 563AD.

Sixty Scottish kings are buried here, despite frequent sackings of the monastery over the centuries by Vikings.

Kings buried here include: **Duncan I**, killed by Macbeth in 1040, **Macbeth** and his son, **Lulach**.

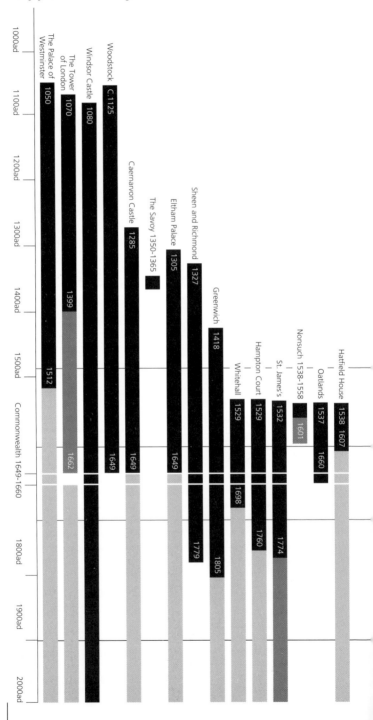

The Palace of Westminster 1050
The Tower of London 1070 · 1399 · 1662
Windsor Castle 1080 · 1649
Woodstock C.1125 · 1649
Caernarvon Castle 1285 · 1649
The Savoy 1350-1365
Eltham Palace 1305 · 1649
Sheen and Richmond 1327 · 1779
Greenwich 1418 · 1805
Whitehall 1529 · 1698
Hampton Court 1529 · 1760
St. James's 1532 · 1774
Nonsuch 1538-1558 · 1601
Oatlands 1537 · 1660
Hatfield House 1538 · 1607
1512

Commonwealth 1649-1660

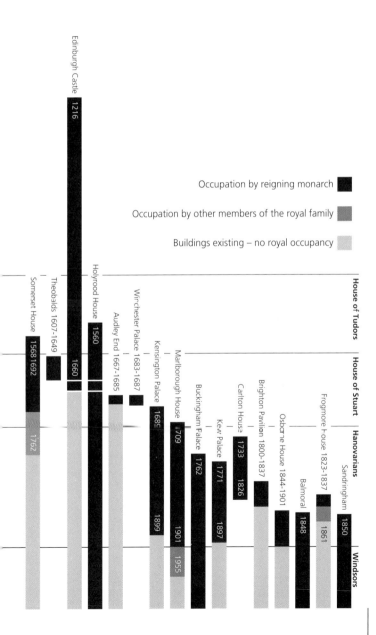

Medieval Monarchs

House of Tudors

House of Stuart

Hanovarians

Windsors

Occupation by reigning monarch

Occupation by other members of the royal family

Buildings existing – no royal occupancy

Edinburgh Castle 1216

Somerset House 1568 1692 1762

Theobalds 1607-1649

Holyrood House 1560 1660

Audley End 1667-1685

Winchester Palace 1683-1687

Kensington Palace 1689 1899

Marlborough House 1709 1901 1955

Buckingham Palace 1762

Kew Palace 1771 1897

Carlton House 1733 1826

Brighton Pavilion 1800-1837

Osborne House 1844-1901

Frogmore House 1823-1837

Balmoral 1848 1861

Sandringham 1850

Appendices **Kings & Queens of England**

ANGLO-SAXON MONARCHS
Canute 1016-1035
Canute established Danish rule in England and he brought increased trade and prosperity to the country.

Harold I 1035-1040 & **Hardecanute** 1040-1042
Harold was the illegitimate son of Canute and ruled after his father's death in 1040. His half-brother, Hardecanute, succeeded him. Hardecanute was the son of Canute's second marriage to Emma of Normandy.

Edward the Confessor 1042-1066
Son of Elthelred the Unready and Emma of Normandy. A Saxon king, he won victories over the Danes. He was cousin of William of Normandy and a brother-in-law of Harold II. Their dispute over the inheritance of the English throne led to the Norman Conquest.

Harold II 1066
Harold was the last Saxon king of England. As Earl of Wessex and East Anglia, he held much power during the reign of Edward the Confessor and declared himself king on Edward's death.
   Harold ruled for only nine months before his defeat by William of Normandy.

HOUSE OF NORMANDY
William I 1066-1087   21
William the Conqueror became king after his victory at Hastings in 1066. He regularised the country's administration and established a taxation system based on the 'Domesday' book.
   He spent most of his time in Normandy, where he died in 1087.

William II 1087-1100   13
Named Rufus after his reddish skin, he was the third son of the Conqueror. He spent much of his reign trying to gain control of Normandy, inherited by his elder brother. This he succeeded in doing, but was soon killed whilst hunting, leaving the throne to his younger brother.

Henry I 1100-1135   35
Crowned three days after William's death, Henry ousted his eldest brother from the Dukedom of Normandy six years later.
   Once he gained Normandy, he was rarely in England during his thirty year reign.

HOUSE OF ANJOU
Matilda 1135 & Stephen 1135-54   19

Though Matilda was the daughter of Henry I, she was ousted from the throne in favour of her cousin, Stephen. His reign was troubled when she invaded and civil war began.

 After Matilda returned to France, her son (later Henry II) defeated Stephen.

Henry II 1154-1189   35
With his accession, England became part of an empire stretching through France to the Spanish border.

Richard I 1189-1199   10
The third son of Henry I was better known as Richard the Lionheart. He ruled England for ten years but only spent six months in the country. His time, and the country's money, were taken up with the crusades.

John 1199-1216   17
John was the younger brother of Richard I. During his reign, he lost the dukedom of Normandy and other inherited lands in France.

 In England, his rule was marked by unrest with the barons.

Henry III 1216-1272   56 + 19 days
John's eldest son succeeded to the throne when only nine. During his reign, the King's Council became known as Parliament.

Edward I 1272-1307   35
Edward was on a crusade when he inherited his father's throne but took four years to return to England. During his rule Wales and Scotland were invaded.

Edward II 1307-1327   20
Edward's reign was troubled by both Scottish and French invasions. He abdicated and was later murdered.

Edward III 1327-1377   50
Edward ruled England for over fifty years, during which time he established parliament at Westminster. He saw English replace French as the national language. He also took possession of Calais.

Richard II 1377-1399   22
The grandson of Edward III came to the throne when young and his uncle, the Duke of Lancaster, effectively ruled. Richard surrendered the throne to the duke's son, Henry Bolingbroke, in 1399.

HOUSE OF LANCASTER
Henry IV 1399-1413   14
Henry's reign was taken up with suppressing revolts and uprisings from rival factions including the House of York.

RICHARD III

MARY I

Henry V 1413-1422

The second Lancastrian king died in France, where he had spent most of his reign fighting for land. In 1415 at the Battle of Agincourt he reconquered Normandy.

Henry VI 1422-1461 & 1470-1471

He was only nine months old when he became king. During his rule, the rivalry between two factions became known as the War of the Roses.

HOUSE OF YORK
Edward IV 1461-1470 & 1471-1783

Edward encouraged trade, particularly in wool, which lead to the country's increased wealth.

Edward V 1483

Son of Edward IV, he lived at Ludlow Castle in Wales during his 77 day reign. He was murdered the day before his coronation at the Tower of London and his uncle, Richard, Duke of Gloucester became king.

Richard III 1483-85

Popular history condemns him, although he launched significant financial reforms that boosted trade.

HOUSE OF TUDOR
Henry VII 1485-1509

The War of the Roses ended with his reign. Henry set England on course to become a major European power through powerful trade and marriage alliances.

Henry VIII 1509-1547

Son of Henry VII, he established the Church of England after the break with Roman Catholicism. He suppressed 823 monasteries and centralised administrative power in the monarch. Henry built a powerful navy of 53 war ships.

Edward VI 1547-1553   6

During Edward's minority reign, his Lord Protector was the Duke of Northumberland, who reinforced Protestantism in England.

Mary I 1553-1558   5

She came to the throne after the nine-day reign of Northumberland's daughter-in-law, Lady Jane Grey. Mary was the first undisputed female sovereign in England. She restored Catholicism. England lost Calais, its last European possession, during her reign.

Elizabeth I 1558-1603

Elizabeth re-established the Protestant Church of England. She supported a growth in the arts, particularly literature, and stimulated trade. When her navy defeated the Spanish Armada in 1558, England vied to become the leading power in Europe.

HOUSE OF STUART

James I 1603-1625 (**James VI** of Scotland)   22

The second cousin of Elizabeth, his reign unified the crowns of Scotland and England.

   In 1607, the first North American colony was established at Jamestown, Virginia

Charles I 1625-1649   24

Charles was a strong patron of the arts, particularly painting. His autocratic style of rule led to the Civil War of 1642-1651.

COMMONWEALTH 1649-1660

After victory by the Parliamentary Forces under Oliver Cromwell, England was declared a Commonwealth and Cromwell the Lord Protector.

Charles II 1660-1685   25

Son of Charles I, he restored the splendour of the monarchy. The arts were stimulated after their suppression during the Commonwealth. Much of London was rebuilt after the Great Fire of 1666.

James II 1685-1688

Brother of Charles II, James's conversion to Catholicism lost him popularity and led to his overthrow by Protestants in the Glorious Revolution of 1688. He was exiled and died near Versailles in France in 1701, having lived to see both his daughters succeed to the throne in England.

GEORGE IV

ELIZABETH II

William III 1689-1702 & **Mary II** 1689-1694 13 & 5

William was the son of Charles I's sister and a cousin of Mary, who was the eldest daughter of James II.

   The joint monarchs established Protestant rule through the Bill of Rights which also curbed royal powers. William won significant victories in Ireland. Mary introduced Dutch tastes to domestic design.

Anne 1702-1714 12

Anne was the second daughter of James II and was married to Prince George of Denmark.

   She saw the Act of Union in 1707 join the English and Scottish Parliaments. During her reign, England emerged as the dominant European power with John Churchill's military victories in south Germany. He was awarded with the dukedom of Marlborough.

HOUSE OF HANOVER

George I 1714-1727 13

George inherited the crown through his mother, Sophia, a Protestant granddaughter of James I. He survived the first Scottish Stuart rebellion in 1715.

George II 1727-1760 33

The son of George I was the last king to lead troops into battle, at Dettingen in 1743. He relied heavily on powerful ministers and his reign saw agricultural and industrial advances leading to great social changes. He defeated the last Catholic threat in the 1745 Stuart Revolt and extended England's power into Europe, America and India.

George III 1760-1820 60 SA yrst 3marths

The grandson of George II. During his long reign the population doubled. Despite increase in power elsewhere, the American colonies were lost in 1782.

REGENCY 1811-1820

The eldest son of George III was made Prince Regent when his father was declared mad.

George IV 1820-1830   10

As Prince Regent from 1811, he effectively reigned for nineteen years. His profligate lifestyle damaged the monarch's moral strength, but he was a strong patron of the arts and architecture.

William IV 1830-1837   7

Brother of George IV. In 1837, the Reform Act reflected the shift of political power from the monarch and aristocracy to the emerging industrial classes.

Victoria 1837-1901   63 yrs 7 mths

The niece of William IV. Her reign saw the height of British power: she ruled over a quarter of the world's land mass and population. Victoria set a tone of high moral standards but saw the monarchy lose power and become a ceremonial symbol.

HOUSE OF WINDSOR (CHANGED FROM SAXE-COBURG-GOTHA IN 1917)

Edward VII 1901-1910   9

The eldest son of Victoria restored much of the splendour of monarchy after his mother's years of seclusion. His reign saw the growing tension between Germany and the other European powers.

George V 1910-1936   26

Son of Edward VII. George saw Britain successfully through the First World War and the financial crises of the 1920s and 1930s. He maintained stability when many monarchs throughout the world lost their throne.

Edward VIII 1936

Eldest son of George V. A popular Prince of Wales, Edward left the monarchy scandalised to marry an American divorcee.

George VI 1936-1952   15 yrs 2 mths

Brother of Edward VIII. George re-established the dignity of the monarchy during the Second World War. In 1945, the victorious Labour Government introduced the welfare state. By the end of his reign, the British Empire was no more, though most of the countries within it had formed the Commonwealth of Nations, with the king as head.

Elizabeth II 1952-

The eldest daughter of George VI has led the monarchy through massive social and political changes which have at times questioned the institution's very need to exist.

Appendices **Heraldry**

Formalised heraldry dates from 1066 and is granted by the monarch, the 'source of all honour'. Before the ability to read was common, heraldry was often the clearest way to distinguish a member of the monarchy or aristocracy, when possessions would be marked with their individual designs.

The Royal Standard

Today the Royal Standard is the most obvious example of heraldry.

Through the centuries, the flag has changed many times. Each change reflected the individual monarch and the varying possessions of the Crown.

For example, from 1300 through to 1800, English claims on land in France were symbolised by a lily; and in the eighteenth century, a horse represented the Hanoverian dynasty.

The present flag was created for Victoria in 1837.

The Royal Standard is the personal flag of the monarch and is flown wherever the Queen is present.

The Standard is made of four panels, in the colours of blue, yellow and red:

■ two red panels, each with three gold lions. They represent England and date from Richard I in the twelfth century.

■ a blue panel with the yellow harp represents Ireland. It dates from James I in the seventeenth century.

■ a yellow panel with a red standing lion represents Scotland. This was incorporated when the Scottish James VI became King of England.

Note

In Scotland, the Royal Standard is different: the red standing lion of Scotland is represented on two yellow panels, and the English gold lions on one.

Royal Badges

In addition to the flags, each monarch would have one or two animals that would symbolise his or her reign. These would also be used to mark the Crown's properties and can be seen on the facades and entrances to royal residences. (See **Pub Names**)

Appendices **Pub names**

Many pubs are named after the royal badges. This happens most often when the pub is close to royal property and was used for overfill accommodation. The names often refer to the reign in which the pub was built, for example:

THE GEORGE & DRAGON (Patron Saint of England: became popular as emblem of the Knights of the Garter of 1360s)

THE WHITE HART (Richard II)

THE SWAN (Henry IV)

THE ANTELOPE & RED LION (House of Lancaster, Henry V)

THE BULL or **WHITE LION** (Edward IV)

THE HIND (Edward V)

THE WHITE BOAR, BLUE BOAR or **TWO BOARS** (Richard III)

THE ROSE & CROWN, PORTCULLIS or **WELSH RED DRAGON** (House of Tudor)

THE DRAGON (Henry VIII)

THE GREYHOUND (Henry VIII or Edward VI)

THE EAGLE (Mary I)

THE UNICORN (Scottish Stuarts)

THE GEORGE (Hanoverian Kings)

The royal family have long ceased using pubs for accommodation. However names continue to commemorate them. **THE CROWN** is the most popular name for over a thousand pubs; also **THE LION** which symbolises England and was often used in conjunction with the animal of a particular monarch.

THE SWAN ON BAYSWATER ROAD, LONDON

Appendices **The Royal Year**

The Queen's year is very structured and its pattern remains almost unchanged since she came to the throne in 1952.

During the year, she attends around 400 events in Britain. Most of these are unpublicised and poorly attended; some are private. However, there are regular events in the calendar, where she can be seen.

January
■ The Queen finishes her Christmas holiday at **SANDRINGHAM**, Norfolk. She attends St Mary Margaret's Church each Sunday.

February, March & April
■ The Queen returns to London and divides her time between **BUCKINGHAM PALACE** and **WINDSOR CASTLE**.

■ If there are any Royal Overseas Tours, this is the time of year when they are planned.

■ The Queen celebrates her Accession to the throne on February 6th, with gun salutes at **HYDE PARK** and the **TOWER OF LONDON**.

Easter
■ The Queen gives the traditional gift of money to the poor at the ancient Maundy Service at **WESTMINSTER ABBEY** on the Monday following Easter.

May
■ She attends the **ROYAL WINDSOR HORSE SHOW**.

■ In late May, the Queen goes to the Chelsea Flower Show in the grounds of the **CHELSEA ROYAL HOSPITAL**.

■ Any visits from foreign Heads of State usually take place at this time. During this time, **THE MALL** is lined with the Union Jack flag and that of the visiting country.

June
■ The traditional English 'Season' opens on the first Saturday of the month when she attends the **EPSOM DERBY**.

■ She takes the salute during the **TROOPING OF THE COLOUR**, London for her official birthday as Queen (anniversary of coronation). The Queen leaves **BUCKINGHAM PALACE** at 10.40am, passing down the Mall to reach **HORSE GUARDS PARADE** twenty minutes later. After the hour-long ceremony, she returns to Buckingham Palace, where the royal family watch the Royal Air Force flyover at 1.00pm on the balcony.

■ She attends the Service of the Order of Garter at St George's Chapel, **WINDSOR CASTLE**.

■ She drives through Windsor Great Park in an open carriage to attend the **ROYAL ASCOT** Race Meeting.

July
■ **Royal Henley Regatta**, Oxfordshire, started in 1839, is frequently attended by the Duke of Edinburgh.
■ 8,000 are invited to attend the three Garden Parties in the grounds of **Buckingham Palace**.
■ The Queen attends the traditional Royal Tournament at **Earls Court**, London
■ As Commander-in-Chief of the Armed Forces she takes the Sovereign's Parade at **Sandhurst Military College**, Camberley, Surrey.
■ The Queen attends race meetings at **Goodwood**, Sussex.

August & September
■ The Queen goes to Scotland, where she carries out her duties as Scottish monarch and stays at **Holyroodhouse Palace** in Edinburgh.
■ She is joined by the whole royal family for the annual summer holiday at **Balmoral**.
■ The Queen attends the annual Highland Games at **Braemar Castle**.

October & November
■ The Queen returns to London, residing at **Buckingham Palace** and **Windsor Castle** for weekends.
■ She reads the Queen's Speech at the **State Opening of Parliament**, which outlines the Government's schedule of legislation.
■ On November 5th, she attends the Festival of Remembrance at **the Cenotaph**, Whitehall.

December
■ The royal family gather for the Christmas holidays at **Sandringham**, Norfolk.

The Queen and Queen Mother arriving at **Royal Ascot**

For further information, see the royal family on the internet: www.royal.gov.uk

Index of Sites

Places in *italics* no longer exist.

Royal Residences & Properties:
castles, palaces & houses

Mischon de Rega Solicitors **51**
Neville Hairdressers **56**
Peat Marwick McLintoch **89**
St Mary's Hospital Paddingon **81**
Vogue House **43**
15 Wyndham Place **81**

Shops: London
Ainsworths **83**
J A Allen **55**
Anderson & Sheppard **44**
Asprey **43**
Berry Brothers **22**
John Boyd **66**
Cartier **43**
Collingwood **43**
Corney & Barrow **89**
Dege & Sons **44**
Ede & Ravenscroft **51**
J Floris **23**
Fogal **43**
Fortnum & Mason **45**
Garrards **45**
General Trading Company **67**
Gieves & Hawkes **44**
Hamleys **45**
Harrods **66**
Harvey Nichols **66**
Hatchards **45**
Hawes & Curtis **23**
H R Higgins **42**
Hodgkiss & Sons, Berks **134**

Holland & Holland **42**
Johns & Pegg **80**
Kanga Boutique **66**
John Lidstone's **55**
David Linley 57, **69**
John Lobb **22**
James Lock **22**
Paul Longmire **22**
Henry Maxwell **41**
Moyses Stephens **67**
Bruce Oldfield **66**
Paxton & Whitfield **23**
Penhaligon **45**
Henry Poole **44**
Purdey, James & Sons **41**
Janet Reger **66**
Rigby & Peller **66**
Simpsons **45**
Spink & Sons **22**
Stephens Brothers **44**
Swaine, Adeney & Brigg **44**
Anthony Tate **55**
Thresher & Glenny **50**
Trickers **23**
Truefitt & Hill **22**
Turnbull & Asser **23**
Twinings **50**
Catherine Walker **67**
Captain Watts of London **45**
Bernard Weatherill **44**
Whiteleys **74**